GREAT RV TRIPS

REVISED EDITION

GREAT RV TRIPS

REVISED EDITION

A Guide to the Best RV Trips in
the United States, Canada and Mexico

Charles L. Cadieux

Fulcrum Publishing
Golden, Colorado

The information in *Great RV Trips, Revised Edition,* is accurate as of April 1998. However, prices, hours of operation, phone numbers, addresses, and other items change rapidly. If something in the book is incorrect, please write to the author at Fulcrum Publishing, 350 Indiana Street, Suite 350, Golden, Colorado 80401-5093.

Library of Congress Cataloging-in-Publication Data

Cadieux, Charles L.
    Great RV trips: a guide to the best RV trips in the United States, Canada and Mexico / Charles L. Cadieux.—Rev. ed.
        p.   cm.
    Includes index.
    ISBN 1-55591-327-X (pbk.)
        1. West (U.S.)—Guidebooks.   2. Canada—Guidebooks.   3. Mexico—Guidebooks.   4. Automobile travel—West (U.S.)—Guidebooks.   5. Automobile travel—Canada—Guidebooks.   6. Automobile travel—Mexico—Guidebooks.   7. Recreational vehicles—West (U.S.)   I. Title.
    F590.3.C33   1998
    917.04'539—dc21   98–19086
                                                                          CIP

Printed in Canada
0 9 8 7 6 5 4 3 2 1

Fulcrum Publishing
350 Indiana Street, Suite 350
Golden, Colorado 80401-5093
(800) 992-2908 • (303) 277-1623
website: www.fulcrum-books.com
e-mail: fulcrum@fulcrum-books.com

Contents

Preface

Those new to any belief are often the most zealous in seeking out new converts. This is certainly true of converts to the recreational vehicle lifestyle. When we first got our inexpensive tent trailer, we became a nuisance bragging about the freedom and economy of travel. As we slowly worked our way up to bigger and better vehicles, we fell in love with travel in Mexico with our RV; and we decided that it was our duty to introduce others to RVing across the border. For seven years we led caravans of RVs into Mexico and derived great pleasure from showing newcomers how great this experience could be. Travel to Alaska and to the Canadian Maritime Provinces was similar: We did it, we loved it and we led others into doing the same.

For thirty-five years we have enjoyed traveling new routes, seeing new sights, learning new things and, above all, meeting new and interesting people. All in our RV. We believe that there is no limit to the enjoyment that can be obtained from RV travel. Through this book, we hope to lead even more people into greater enjoyment of their RVs. Happy RVing!

1
The Recreational Vehicle Lifestyle

What is so attractive about RV travel? Why are there more than 8 million RVs on America's roads today? Why are dealers selling more than 850,000 more RVs every year?

RVing is a way of life. It's freedom from needing reservations, from paying outrageous prices for lousy food at roadside restaurants, from paying too much for second-rate motel accommodations—it's the freedom to go where you want to go, when you want to go there!

Perhaps that's putting too much emphasis on the money end of things. If your real reason for buying an RV is to save money, you're limited to pop-up trailers or pickup campers. The initial investment in the larger types has to be amortized over a long period of regular use, or you'll never recover that initial investment. My solution to that problem is to keep my motor coach on the road.

Consider many factors before deciding to buy your first RV! Remember that your big RV will probably get 8 to 10 miles per gallon—while your new car may get over 32 miles to the gallon. If you drive 350 miles per day, the car will use 11 gallons of gasoline, the RV will devour 44 gallons. At today's prices, that's a saving for the car of about $36, but that $36 won't pay for one night in a motel in most areas. Of course, in your RV you will have to pay from $13 to $19 to camp one night, which will make the motel room more economical. But you don't have to carry your suitcases into a motel room; all your things are right where you want them—convenient and familiar—and that's worth a lot. In the campground, you seldom have to listen to the noise of a party next door—and you never have to suffer the smell of stale tobacco smoke.

One of my closest friends has a habit of enjoying a bowl of ice cream before going to bed. In his motor coach he simply dishes up the ice cream from his own refrigerator; in a motel he has to get dressed, drive a half mile to the Baskin Robbins and pay twice as much for the same ice cream. In his personal accounting, this is one of the major reasons for buying a motor coach.

Another friend with years of experience RVing tells me that the nicest thing is simply knowing where his bathroom is and not having to stop and ask for the key at a filling station.

When I got my first RV, the main attraction was not having to unload a tent and set it up each night, then take it down each morning. Now, thirty-five years later, the main attractions are convenience and freedom—freedom to go where

I want to go, camp where I want to camp and not have to load or unload anything; everything I need is right there in its normal place—every time.

We tend to think of the recreational vehicle as something new, and it really is only about seventy years old. But the idea of a traveling home is ancient and today's RVs owe much to their predecessors.

Thirty years ago, I was privileged to inspect the "sheepwagon" used by Basque sheepherders on the plains of Wyoming. These men came from the Catalan part of Spain and signed up to herd sheep twenty-four hours a day, seven days a week for a year or two before taking their savings and returning to Spain. Most of them used a team of horses to pull their "wagon" to the sheep pastures, where their only company for weeks at a time was their sheepdog. The wagon was merely a sturdy canvas-topped wooden box, but the interior was a model of the efficient use of space.

There was a comfortable mattress bed, a wood- or coal-burning stove for heating and cooking and, most surprising to me, a retractable table that disappeared into the wall when not in use but which was exceedingly stable when extended.

Under the bed were built-in drawers and storage compartments that held the shepherd's food supplies and his clothing as well as his cooking and eating utensils. Granted, there was nothing luxurious about it, but it was nonetheless a very practical and comfortable traveling home.

Long before the time of the Basque sheepherders, nomadic peoples in Asia used "yurts," small compact homes mounted on two-wheeled carts drawn by horses or oxen. The walls and roof were made of hides or pressed felt, depending upon local custom. There was no real door, just an overlapping layer of hide to keep out the icy winds that blew across the steppes. Their only heat came from an inside fire contained in a rude brazier with the smoke vented out through a hole in the tentlike roof. This was the way of life of the Mongols, the nomadic horsemen who ruled most of the known world under Genghis Khan. These pastoral nomads traveled great distances between summer and winter pastures, and the yurt had to be efficient.

The beginnings of the "home on wheels" in the United States was less primitive. Yankees have always been known as tinkerers, as people who loved to figure out solutions to problems. One problem was how to travel by automobile without the expense of hotels and restaurants. The solution was to build an "autocamp" or a "housecar" as the first ones were known. A modified car or truck chassis accommodated a boxy structure that housed a bed and a stove and even—on rare occasions—a toilet.

As the U.S. system of highways grew and improved in quality, interest in "autocamping" grew along with it, and when the RV first went into commercial production it met with great success. That success is proven by the overwhelming array of RVs on the market today.

Let's consider each type of RV and discuss its advantages and disadvantages. Least expensive is the pop-up or "tent" trailer. This is a light, easily towed vehicle that opens up into a full-sized room with sleeping room for four. They range from the very simplest, providing only sleeping space on a pad mattress and some storage, up to the luxurious models featuring stove, icebox or 12-volt refrigerator and even a toilet. I've owned three in my day and can attest to the fact that they offer a surprising amount of room because the beds fold down from the trailer walls, leaving the middle free. They tow very easily—so easily that you're apt to forget that the trailer is behind you, as I did when I parked in Pinedale, Wyoming—diagonal parking—and almost blocked the entire street. Disadvantages include the problem of setting up and taking down in inclement weather, and the fact that they are difficult to heat in cold weather. During extended periods of rain, they are apt to get damp and musty. In fair weather, however, they are an inexpensive and very satisfactory way to RV.

Next lowest in price is the pickup camper, a miniature motor home built to slide into the box of a three-quarter-ton pickup truck. Don't put one on a half-ton truck—it's too much of a load. Most pickup campers provide a double bed in the "cab-over" section of the camper, which makes a very comfortable bed, wide enough to sleep two comfortably. In most pickup campers, there is a dinette section that uses the tabletop as a part of the bed so that the dinette converts into another bed for two. Most of these dinette beds end up being a bit short for the adult male but are just fine for children.

The pickup camper also includes a convenient propane stove, usually with three or four burners, that is permanently mounted atop a small oven. Most pickup campers have a double sink for washing dishes and carry at least 35 gallons of fresh water. Some, not all, have propane furnaces to take the chill off. Add a good-sized refrigerator with a freezer compartment, and you're in business.

Way back in 1967 my wife and I and our two teenage girls made a 6,700-mile trek through Mexico in a Huntsman pickup camper, and we were very comfortable. Most of the time the two youngsters rode in the cab-over bed where they could see out the big front window. This worked fine until we drove through the Thousand Peaks area near Mexico City. This winding road threatened motion sickness for the girls in the "catbird" seat, so they came down and shared the pickup cab with us. If someone usually rides in the camper unit, make sure that your rig has an intercom to allow for two-way communications. Strangely enough, without an intercom it is very difficult for those in the camper to attract the attention of the driver when underway.

There are many advantages to the pickup camper idea. First of all, it's low priced in comparison with a trailer or motor coach. Second, the camper can be removed, freeing up the truck for normal use. In fact, the camper can usually be made into a free-standing vacation headquarters, on its own legs, while you use the pickup truck for other purposes. Third, the pickup camper is agile and can go anywhere a car can go. Finally, it's great for RVers who want to tow and launch a boat. We spent five very happy years tooling around the country in ours.

Moving a bit farther up the economic scale, we come to the trailer, which can range from a tiny 12-foot cocoon to sleep two, all the way up to a luxurious 33-foot aluminum castle. A 27-foot trailer affords more living space than does a 27-foot motor coach, simply because much of the motor coach space is taken up by the engine. Most trailers mount their propane bottle or bottles on the front tow bar, outside the trailer, which also saves space.

Obviously, a trailer costs far less than a motor coach, but the trailer can't move by itself, and so you have to figure in the cost of the tow vehicle. It's not a wise idea to scrimp here! Towing a trailer is heavy work and requires a powerful, stable tow vehicle. The Chevrolet Suburban has established a fine record for itself in this regard and makes an excellent tow vehicle. So do the heavy three-quarter-ton pickup trucks by GMC, Chevrolet, Ford and Dodge.

When choosing a tow vehicle, go for the bigger engine every time. GM's 454 and Ford's 460 are good choices. And it's been my experience that the more powerful engines don't use any more gasoline than smaller ones when towing the same load. This is because the bigger engine is loafing most of the time, thus saving gasoline.

The biggest advantage of the trailer is that it offers the most usable space and the most comfort for the dollar. It is also very convenient

for the RVer who goes to a destination and parks the trailer for extended periods. If you're the kind of RVer who makes extended trips, parking each night in a different campground, it becomes something of a nuisance to have to unhook and level up every night. Also, some drivers can park a trailer easily; others have the devil's own time learning how to back a trailer into a parking space. Before you decide on a trailer, try your hand at backing one into a space.

When considering a trailer, think about the possibility of a Hi-Lo trailer, which can be lowered to less than tow vehicle height when moving and cranked up to full height when parked for the night. Decide for yourself whether you like the idea.

My biggest complaint with the trailer is that most of them aren't equipped with a strong enough suspension to handle their weight. In traveling the rough roads of Mexico, I found that while trailers made up only about 25 percent of our caravan, they accounted for more than 75 percent of the "lost time" problems. Broken springs were the most common problem, with tire and wheel failures a close second. They simply did not have enough backbone in their springs. Check this out when shopping for trailers. Also check the electric braking system and make sure it is adequate to handle the load so that your trailer won't goose your tow vehicle in the rear every time you hit the brakes.

We move up now from the simple trailer to the "fifth wheel" type of trailer. This system—which carries some of the weight on a special gooseneck tongue anchored in the middle of the wheelbase of your tow vehicle—changes lots of things. Because some of the trailer length is "over" the pickup truck that tows it, you can have more living space without increasing the total length of trailer and tow vehicle. The pickup tow vehicle, however, loses some of its truck bed space because of the gooseneck being mounted far in front of the ball hitch area.

To me, an attractive feature of the fifth wheeler is the wonderful bedrooms they offer, reached by climbing three or four steps up from the trailer floor into the front part of the trailer that rides over the pickup truck. The nicest bedroom layouts in any RVs are found in fifth wheelers. But wonderful floor plans can be found in either configuration, so find what you like and give it a try.

All other things being equal, the fifth wheeler and tow vehicle is shorter than a trailer and similar tow vehicle. This makes towing easier, with less tendency to fishtail. Again, as with the straight trailer route, the prospective fifth wheeler purchaser

should take the rig for a drive, in traffic and on the back roads, uphill and around sharp curves. See if you're cut out to drive such a rig, and by all means practice backing into a trailer space—the fifth wheeler backs very differently than a trailer. I remember one fellow who absolutely could *not* back up his fifth wheeler. We were on a Mexican caravan and the solution was easy—every time we came to a new trailer park, another caravaner, a friend of his, took over and smoothly backed the fifth wheeler into its assigned space.

The next type of RV to consider is the motor coach. Here the number of choices is so great that it is almost mind-boggling. You can buy a micro motor coach on an underpowered Japanese import truck for as little as $23,000, and you can spend $250,000 (that's right, a quarter of a million dollars) for a 40-foot deluxe coach with a rear-engine diesel, ice maker, garbage compactor, rearview TV camera that allows you to see directly behind the coach, two roof air conditioners, two television receivers, a roof-mounted satellite dish, classy stereo, CD and tape player—the list of extras goes on and on, and they all go *on* the price tag.

Disadvantages of the motor coach are its high purchase cost, its low miles per gallon and the fact that the motor takes up some of your space. There is a rule of RVing: The need for storage space in every RV expands to exceed the space available.

Now let us talk about gasoline mileage. I once drove my rig behind an identical rig driven by another—we filled up at the same stations, drove exactly the same speed and covered the same distance—and he reported that he got 13.5 miles per gallon while I only got 8.3 miles per gallon. This happened so often that I finally figured out that the only difference between him and me was that I was telling the truth. Sneaking a look at his pump readings told me that he was buying the same number of gallons as I was. Why is it that some folks who go to church regularly, are good to their families and don't cheat on their income tax feel compelled to tell outrageous lies about something so trivial as their gas mileage? Again, the bigger, more powerful engine will not increase your gasoline costs—usually the opposite is true. I sold a 23-foot coach with a 350 motor and replaced it with a 31-footer with a 454 motor—and got *better* mileage.

Actually, there are many different kinds of motor coach. The Class A coach is the largest, with the coach built from scratch, right on the bare frame of a specially designed chassis. Class A motor homes, or motor coaches, offer everything you need to live comfortably, even for full-timers.

The Class B coach, also called a van camper, is a van with a few amenities added. Usually, these amenities consist of a bed and a small kitchen, sometimes with a toilet and a raised roof to allow for standing room. To my mind, they are the worst possible compromise as they do not allow for comfortable fully contained living and cost very nearly as much as a comparable Class A motor coach.

Class C is another matter entirely. There are really two classes of Class C coaches, grouped according to size. The smallest is the micro-mini, which is built on the stretched frame of a small truck. Most popular have been the stretched Nissans and Toyotas. The manufacturer saws the longitudinal members of the frame across and inserts a "stretch" piece of frame to make the chassis long enough to accommodate a very small motor coach. I've never owned one, but I have driven several on long-distance tests to form my own opinion. Gas mileage was exceptionally good in the ones I tested, but they seemed underpowered and required a lot of downshifting when pulling much of a grade.

Obviously, the micro-mini cannot offer the usable space of its larger competitors, but gas mileage is a definite attraction. Before you buy one, rent one and take it on the road for a week or two to see if you're comfortable with what it has to offer.

The slightly larger type of Class C is built on a modified van chassis. Most of these are quite comfortable, providing all the amenities except extra living space and extra storage room. I know one couple who lived—full time—in their 20-foot Class C while they traveled over all of North America. They go north in the springtime and south in the fall and are wondrously content with their life. Says Laura, "The hardest thing is to get in the habit of getting rid of things you don't need right now instead of saving them and tucking them into every nook and cranny of the coach."

So which type of RV is for you? It depends upon what kind of RV travel you'll be doing and how much money you want to invest in your RV.

If you plan to travel to a fixed destination and park there comfortably for a two-week vacation, you can't beat the trailer or the fifth wheeler.

If your RVing is like ours, with lots of driving and lots of one- to three-day stops at different destinations, your obvious choice is a motor coach—size to be determined by your budget.

Are you going to be towing a boat? Your best choice then is a pickup camper or a motor coach. Some states allow you to pull a boat behind a trailer that is pulled by a pickup or van. It may be legal, but it just ain't right. That type of rig is impossible for the average driver to back up. It requires extreme care in entering and exiting gas stations, and it is the cause of many accidents. Pulling one vehicle behind your tow vehicle is enough—pulling two vehicles is a dangerous practice that should be illegal.

Do you plan to explore the back roads of Mexico? Then go for the pickup camper for its agility and ability to do without a lot of things and still deliver good mileage and creature comfort.

Here are some suggestions, gleaned from a lifetime of RVing, leading RVs to Guatemala and Alaska, from the Cape Breton Highlands in Nova Scotia to the tip of the Baja Peninsula.

1. No matter which type you choose, it has to have a motor. Don't scrimp on the size of that motor. Underpowered rigs are a constant source of irritation and a safety hazard because they limit your ability to react quickly in a driving emergency.

2. No matter which type suits you best, rent before you buy! Take the rig out for a two-week test run; you'll discover whatever you might object to—things you might never have thought of before.

3. The gray water—from your shower and kitchen sink—and the black water from your toilet must be disposed of. Check into the location of the dump valves. Do you have to get down on your hands and knees to dump the holding tank? Do you want to do that a thousand times? Is it easy to rinse the holding tanks after dumping them?

4. Does the rig you're testing sway whenever a big semi meets you or passes you? This can be dangerous, and reduction of such sway is almost impossible. Dual rear wheels help a lot in minimizing sway; a high profile increases sway.

5. Many coaches now feature greatly enlarged "basement" storage. Do you need that storage? Some people carry all their canned goods down below, but do you really *need* all that space? Remember the rule that the need for storage expands to exceed the space available (I know a guy who carries a kayak in his basement storage). If your coach is a 20-footer, you'll want more storage space. If your coach is a 40-footer with a basement, you'll still want more space. But do you need it? It costs money, you know.

6. Diesel or gasoline power? Diesel engines cost a lot more to buy but they cost a lot less to operate and last far longer. Take your pencil or calculator and figure out how many miles you'll have to drive and multiply that times the economy of the diesel and figure out whether or not you'll *ever* recover the higher initial purchase cost of the diesel, which can be as much as $2,500. I've never owned a diesel, and I know almost nothing about diesel engines—fellow RVers who operate diesels usually swear by them.

7. Now, please allow me to repeat the best advice. Take your chosen type of RV out for a two-week trial (rental) before signing your name on that sales contract. This is the only way to "look before you leap."

After you've decided which type of RV you want to buy, start looking for bargains. Remember that there is a big mark-up in price between what dealers pay and what they charge the customer. Because they sell far fewer units than automobile dealers, RV dealers must get more profit per unit sold. If they didn't get this large mark-up, they'd soon be out of business. But your dealer doesn't have to make *all* of his or her annual profit on you. Just knowing that there's a big mark-up in price should give you the incentive to start bargaining with the dealer.

Do a lot of shopping. It might be worth your while to travel to nearby towns to see what that same rig is selling for elsewhere.

The next question is whether to buy new or previously owned. There is a "new smell" in a brand new coach that's a big attraction to many buyers. But the average motor coach goes down in value at least $5,000 the instant it's driven off the salesroom floor. Used coaches are big bargains, if you're careful. This applies to fifth wheelers and trailers and pickup campers more than it does to coaches. With these vehicles you can see everything and test out everything. With a motor coach you can carefully examine everything *except* the engine. Unless you're a first-class mechanic, you can't really tell what kind of shape the engine is in. It's hard to get away from the feeling that there must be something wrong or it wouldn't be offered for sale so cheaply. If it's so great, how come the owner is selling it?

Nevertheless, you should definitely consider a previously owned rig when you go shopping for your RV, for the very simple reason that you are apt to save thousands compared to the new vehicle price. Look them over carefully, and remember, "If it sounds too good to be true, it usually *is* too good to be true."

The best RV buy I ever made was a 31-foot Southwind motor coach with 22,000 miles on the odometer. Now, with 83,000 miles on the odometer, I'm beginning to think I made a very good deal.

There are many reasons why RVs in good shape, seemingly brand new, are offered for sale. Why did the original owners part with them? In many cases, they didn't follow my advice to rent one first. When they got their dream RV, they found out that they didn't even like this form of travel so they got rid of it.

Other purchasers spent a lot of money for a rig, then found out that they didn't use it enough to justify keeping it, so they sold it at a big loss. If you get one of these, you're a big winner. One acquaintance of mine, with more money than he needs, bought a brand new gasoline-powered big Beaver coach for $119,000. Then he found out that his best buddy had an even bigger rig, with a diesel pusher. Not to be outdone, my friend bought the bigger model's twin, also with a diesel pusher. He then put his $119,000 rig on the market, asking $99,000. Six months later he sold it for $89,000, and the buyer got a great bargain—a wonderful, almost new motor home for $30,000 less than it cost new.

I've known many RVers who've never bought a new vehicle. Instead they've shopped around and always bought previously owned rigs. One friend has bought used models six times over the past twenty-five years. He figures he's saved enough money to put his two boys through college.

The RV life is a wonderful thing. It is the source of many great friendships, the magic carpet that allows you to visit places you couldn't afford otherwise. It is something that I heartily recommend. But let me repeat two warnings about buying an RV:

1. *Rent one first* and take a two-week spin in it.
2. Do a lot of shopping for both new and used vehicles before you reach for your checkbook.

Recreational vehicle travel is a wonderful way to live—9 million RVers cannot be wrong. But before you head out on your own greatest RV trips, choose wisely—you'll be driving or towing it for quite a few years.

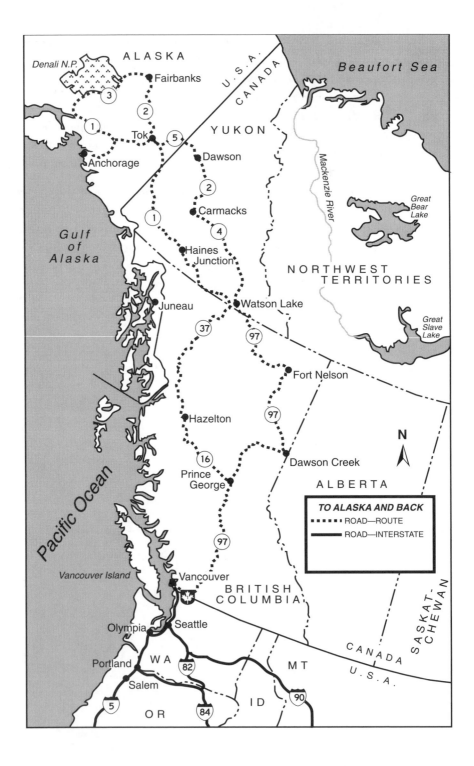

2
To Alaska and Back

The trip to Alaska and back by recreational vehicle is not only the greatest of all RV trips, but a good case can be made for calling it the first, second and third best trip ever to be taken in your RV. You see, there are now many ways to go to Alaska—the Great Land. You can drive the beautiful but interminable Alaskan highway from Dawson Creek, British Columbia, to Alaska and go home via the same road. You can drive the Alaskan Highway up and take the seagoing ferry back to southern British Columbia or even to Seattle, or you can reverse the procedure—go up by sea and return by land. You can drive the famed Cassiar Highway (No. 37) through British Columbia and some of the most beautiful territory on earth and join up with the Alaskan Highway just west of Watson Lake, to continue up the road to Alaska. Then return by the Alaskan or by boat.

There are countless other combinations. For example, you can also leave the Alaskan Highway at Watson Lake and drive the Campbell Highway to connect with the Klondike Highway at Carmacks and continue up through historic Dawson City, over the well-named Top of the World Highway to enter Alaska east of the town named Chicken.

The condition of the Alaskan Highway changes very much from year to year. More and more of it is blacktop, less and less of it is gravel. But that is not always an improvement. A smooth gravel road is much better than a paved one full of potholes. One year the worst tooth-loosener we hit was the stretch inside Alaska from the Canadian border and Tok—the year before that had been a smooth stretch. Spring thaws, mud slides and "frost boils" had taken their destructive toll.

Let's talk a bit about the highway itself. Motivated by the fear that the Japanese might attempt to invade Alaska after their attack upon Pearl Harbor, the U.S. military blasted the road through from Dawson Creek to Fairbanks in 1942, so we could move military forces to Alaska. After great hardship the road was opened to military traffic that same year, but there were sharp turns and grades as steep as 25 percent. In 1943, the road was greatly improved, making it more level and disproving the old adage that a straight line is the shortest distance between two points.

Opened to public travel after World War II, the road became a test of drivers' skill and of RV construction. On my first two trips over the road, twenty years later, I logged 732 miles of gravel road and encountered RVs clad like armored tanks with great screens to protect windshields and headlights from flying rocks and gravel. I completed both trips without even a star on my windshield, but 200 miles into the United States, a passing gravel truck tossed an apple-sized rock and I needed a new windshield.

Oversized gas tanks were needed in the early days, because it was a long way between gas stations. Today, the standard gas tanks that come with your vehicle are plenty big enough, although it is still a good idea to keep the top half of the tank full whenever possible.

Canada sells gasoline by the liter, and you can translate that into imperial gallons, about one and one fifth U.S. gallons. Alaska is a part of the United States, of course, so they use the familiar U.S. gallon. Whether you buy gallons or liters, be prepared to spend considerably more for gasoline than you would in the Lower 48. Lowest prices are found in Anchorage and vicinity; the highest prices I found were at Dawson, in the Yukon Territory.

If you plan on taking the ferry back from Alaska, don't wait until you get up there to buy your ticket. Most ferry sailings are sold out six months to a year in advance.

What should you plan on seeing once you reach Alaska? In my opinion, the following are the absolutely must *see* points, but not in any order of importance.

Denali National Park, formerly called McKinley National Park, is 287 highway miles north of Anchorage, and only 250 miles south of the Arctic Circle. This spectacular park is dominated by North America's tallest mountain, **Mt. McKinley,** which towers 20,320 feet into the Alaskan sky. Big as it is, McKinley's majesty is visible only about 30 percent of the time, as clouds obscure it other times. I've never failed in six trips to see the magnificent spire, but other people have told me that they spent two weeks there and never saw it. Other times it is visible from Anchorage—250 miles away.

Where to camp while visiting Denali?

There's a good KOA at nearby **Healy, Alaska.** The address is P.O. Box 340, Healy, AK 99743. Phone number is (907) 683-2379. Within Alaska, there is a toll-free number: 1-800-478-AKOA. My recommendation is that you make reservations early, in writing, with a check for deposit. Transportation is provided by the KOA to the entrance of Denali National Park, where you can access the shuttle bus which is the only vehicle permitted deep within the park. Tickets for the shuttle bus can be obtained by calling 1-800-622-7275 or (907) 272-7275 locally. This bus stops at the viewpoint on **Polychrome Pass** where you get your first look at magnificent Mt.

McKinley. Further on you can visit **Eielson Visitor Center** and **Wonder Lake.** You can get off anywhere you want, except where grizzlies have recently been sighted, and catch any returning bus that has an empty seat. Grizzly bears are often sighted from the bus, which then stops and allows time for photographs, *but nobody can get off the bus,* for obvious reasons. Once, on the 70-mile run in to Wonder Lake, we photographed nine grizzlies and one big sow just 50 feet from the bus. You almost always see caribou, fox, moose and other animals. Drivers seem to know just how close each animal will allow the bus to come without running off, and drivers have been very cooperative with photographers. RV camping is allowed at **Teklanika** (within the park), but you can expect to wait a week for your camping permit, as it is very popular with visitors. If you prefer a more formal tour of the park than the shuttle bus provides, you can call 1-800-276-7234 for information and reservations. The Tundra Wildlife Tour and a Natural History Tour are two options.

The city of **Valdez,** with its boat trips to the glaciers—especially the giant **Columbia Glacier**—is the terminus of the oil pipeline that begins 800 miles to the north, at Prudhoe Bay on the Arctic Ocean. Oil is an important part of the economy of this beautiful city, and in March 1989, the infamous Exxon *Valdez* ran aground a few miles from the city, spilling 11 million gallons of crude oil. Today, it takes careful inspection to find visible traces of the spill, although the damage to the ecosystem will persist for decades to come. Despite the oil spill, Valdez remains one of the best jumping-off places for salmon and halibut fishing. Valdez sits on the edge of the sea and at the base of the high mountains, giving it claim to the title of Little Switzerland, even though there is nothing little about *any* part of Alaska. Its alpine beauty is reason enough to visit Valdez.

RVs parked at the Portage Glacier. There are good Forest Service campgrounds nearby.

If you want campground information, tickets to visit the glaciers or any other services, you can do it all with one phone call to Valdez at (907) 835-4988. Stan Stephens operates boat charters and cruises and can take you out to see the mighty Columbia close up in a very comfortable craft. You'll cruise right in among the icebergs, watch the seals basking on the ice floes and hear the thunderous cracking sound as an iceberg "calves" into the dark blue waters. He also operates full- and partial-hookup campgrounds right in the harbor area, where the action is always interesting. Full, unmetered hot showers, a coin-operated launderette and clean rest rooms are the big attraction here—along with the spectacular scenery, of course, and the quiet waters of the sound.

Bear Paw RV Park, located on North Harbor Drive overlooking the boat harbor, offers full or partial hookups plus a dump station and coin-operated launderette. We strongly recommend advance reservations, which can be made by phoning (907) 835-2530.

Eagle's Rest RV Park is just outside of town on the Richardson Highway at Pioneer Drive. They claim that you can see no less than eighteen glaciers from your front porch at this campground! That's hard to beat anywhere, but in Alaska you expect the impossible. Full and partial hookups, hot showers without meters and a launderette. Reservations are a good idea in summer months. Write P.O. Box 610, Valdez, AK 99686, or call (907) 835-2373.

If you are on a budget, as most of us are, try the city-operated campground 6 miles from town on the Richardson Highway. It offers more than 100 campsites, water and toilets, but no hookups. Charge is only $5 per day.

Valdez survived the Good Friday earthquake of 1964 and the catastrophic Exxon *Valdez* oil spill of 1989 and remains my favorite city in all of Alaska, a place of mountain beauty, excellent fishing and the home of the unequaled Columbia Glacier.

The **Kenai Peninsula** with special attention to **Ninilchik, Homer** and **Soldotna**—where you'll find the remains of Russian settlement and the world-famous **Kenai Moose Range.** The **Kenai River** is famed for its huge *tyee*, also called king salmon, and for two great runs of red salmon up through the Kenai and into the Russian River. You have to be there at just the right time, however, as the millions of bright red fish speed through on their spawning run, and it lasts only about sixty hours.

The best place to start your tour of the west side of the Kenai Peninsula is at the **Visitor Information Center** in downtown Soldotna. It's open seven days a week from 9:00 A.M. to 7:00 P.M. mid-May through mid-September, (907) 262-1337. But first of all, let's focus on campgrounds to use as headquarters when exploring.

Kenai River Family Campground, at mile 2.2 on Big Eddy Road, offers RV parking right on the bank of the river—and salmon are caught from the bank right there—with electric hookups and water available. They have a good launching ramp into the milk-colored Kenai, and you can arrange boat fishing for kings and silvers. HC 1, P.O. Box 8616, Soldotna, AK 99669, (907) 262-2444.

Kenai Riverbend Campground offers 300 RV spaces with full hookups and 1,600 feet of Kenai River frontage. It also offers a dump station, laundry and showers. P.O. Box 1270, Soldotna, AK 99669, (907) 283-9489.

The eastern side of the same **Kenai Peninsula,** with stops at **Portage Glacier** (good Forest Service campgrounds nearby), the **Seward Highway** (watch for Dall sheep and moose) and **Seward** (with its earthquake museum). While you're in Seward itself, take a boat ride out to the **Kenai Fjords National Park.** In Seward you can park your RV, quite inexpensively, right on the shore where coho salmon can be taken by

The view from the inexpensive ocean-front campground at Seward.

casting from the bank, if the time is right. I did it in mid-August. Incidentally, right where we parked our RVs on the harbor front, the earth opened up during a big earthquake in 1964 and swallowed a bit of the railroad, freight cars and all! But not to worry—it hasn't happened since, although slight tremors are often felt in many parts of Alaska.

The **City of Seward Park and Recreation Department,** Waterfront Park, P.O. Box 167, Seward, AK 99664, (907) 224-4055, offers 22 sites with electric and water hookups and 40 sites without hookups.

Seward's ice-free harbor makes it the entry port for marine traffic. The famed Iditarod dogsled race started here, and it's still the starting point for many seagoing adventures. From Seward, you can take coastal boat trips all over this scenic wonderland, and it is also is a great place to try your hand at deep water

halibut and salmon fishing when the runs are in.

Fairbanks, the city and its surroundings, 1,475 miles from Dawson Creek where the Alaskan Highway begins, started two years before the 1903 gold rush and is now the largest "far northern" city we have (population about 80,000). See the **University of Alaska** with its permafrost research center, goggle at a herd of musk oxen, tour the re-created **Alaskaland Pioneer Park,** ride the paddlewheel steamer on the **Chena** and **Tanana Rivers,** going ashore for a visit to an old settlement. Bring lots of film.

Fairbanks, like many Alaskan towns, is famous for its "salmon bakes." The one at Alaskaland lives up to its billing; it's a good and big feed.

Although the RV season this far north is very short, Fairbanks is better provided with RV parks than any other Alaskan destination. Two of the best are the **Rivers Edge CG,** 4140 Boat Street, Fairbanks, AK 99701, (907) 474-0286 and the **Norlite CG,** 1660 Peger Road, Fairbanks, AK 99701, (907) 474-0206 or within Alaska, 1-800-478-0206. In nearby North Pole, you can find RV spaces at **Roads End RV Park,** 1463 Wescott Lane, North Pole, AK 99705, (907) 488-0295.

These five destinations are the "don't you dare miss 'em" places when planning your Alaskan journey, and if you buy a copy of *The Milepost* you'll have a mile-by-mile log of all the roads you'll cover plus tons of other miscellaneous information. It sells for $18.95 plus $3 shipping and handling from Northwest Books, 22026 20th Avenue Southeast, Bothell, WA 98021. But before you mail off your check to buy this marvelous reference book, check your local discount bookstore. You may find it for only $14.95 and no shipping charge. Its maps and road logs cover all the roads, even the Canadian roads in Alberta, Saskatchewan, British Columbia and the Yukon. *The Milepost* also gives detailed schedules and costs for the ferries on the Inside Passage.

Because you are RVing, you'd better plan to visit **Tok,** which is probably right on your way. It offers what is considered to be the best RV park in the state . It used to be a KOA but is now called **Tok RV Village,** at milepost 1313.4 on the Alaskan Highway. This campground offers 95 spaces with all hookups and 61 pull-through spaces. There's a dump station and an RV wash station that you'll appreciate after traveling through the dusty or muddy sections of the great highway. I once led a caravan of 59 units into this campground and they took care of our needs nicely—of course we had a reservation guaranteed by a deposit.

Tok is pronounced to rhyme with "poke." If you're tired out after driving all the way to Alaska, this might be a good place to loaf for a couple of days and rest up. Gas stations, groceries, hardware, even light RV repairs are available.

Alaska is a grand destination, but getting there can be more than half of the fun. Here's how it went with an organized caravan a few years back.

Day 1:   Got together in **Vancouver, B.C.,** and had a nice salmon bake courtesy of the tour company.

Day 2:   Bus tour of Vancouver.

Day 3:   Drove Vancouver to **Cache Creek,** 200 miles, stayed in Cache Creek CG.

Day 4:   Cache Creek to **Barkerville,** 270 miles. Were treated to "mellerdrammer" and excellent dinner in **Historic Barkerville,** all part of the tour. Primitive camping, no hookups.

Day 5:   Drove Barkerville to **Prince George,** 134 miles. Excellent campsite in Prince George, included in the price of the tour.

Day 6:   Prince George to **Dawson Creek,** the official beginning of the Alaskan Highway; 255 miles today.

Day 7: Bus tour of Dawson Creek, excellent dinner at the Alaska Cafe courtesy of the tour company.

Day 8: Drove Dawson Creek to **Fort Nelson,** a distance of 283 miles. Good campground.

Day 9: Drove only 161 miles today to reach **Muncho Lake,** where we camped without hookups but with the most beautiful lake and mountain views. Quiet, almost perfectly silent except for the far-off call of a loon.

Day 10: Drove 168 miles from Muncho Lake to the city of **Watson Lake,** checked into a very good campground and enjoyed a potluck dinner with fellow caravaners.

Day 11: Drove 280 miles from Watson Lake to **Whitehorse,** capital of the Yukon territory.

Day 12: Enjoyed a boat cruise up the **Yukon River,** with spectacular scenery and rushing waters. In evening went to the Frantic Follies, a Gold Rush era girlie show suitable for the entire family and well received. All part of the tour.

Day 13: Drove 170 miles from Whitehorse to **Minto Landing,** with reserved spaces in a campground with a 1,000-foot frontage on the mighty Yukon River. No hookups, but showers and laundry available.

Day 14: Drove 178 miles from Minto Landing to **Dawson, Yukon Territory,** checked into reserved spaces in small campground, kind of crowded but right downtown within walking distance of everything.

Days 15 and 16:
In Dawson, with paid-for tour of the gold mining area, and a chance to do some gold panning for ourselves at no extra cost to caravaners.

Day 17: Drove an incredibly bad road from Dawson to **Tok, Alaska;** 191 miles of high mountain driving, that started out with a ferry ride across the mighty Yukon. Different time zones on either side of the border.

Day 18: Drove 205 miles from Tok to **Fairbanks,** where you could read the newspaper outdoors twenty-one hours a day in late July. Caravan was treated to show and salmon bake at Alaskaland.

Day 19: In good campground in Fairbanks, were bused to a city tour, lunch at the famous Pumphouse, then a four-hour riverboat tour. Good day.

Day 20: At leisure in Fairbanks.

Day 21: Drove 135 miles from Fairbanks to the KOA at **Healy,** gateway to **Denali National Park.**

Day 22: Bus came to campground and loaded our party for trip through Denali National Park. Saw eleven grizzly bears, eighty Dall sheep, several hundred caribou, four moose, red fox and many other forms of wildlife. Did *not* see Mt. McKinley, which was wreathed in clouds. Day ended with a great salmon bake.

Day 23: Drove 250 miles to the big city of **Anchorage,** parked in city-owned campground.

Day 24: Bus tour of Anchorage, plus stage show and dinner theater, courtesy of the tour company.

Day 25: Drove 235 scenic miles from Anchorage to oceanside campground in **Homer.** Tour company treated us to an "all you can eat" buffet at the Porpoise Room on Homer Spit—excellent fresh halibut and salmon.

Day 26: Free day in Homer. Many caravaners went halibut fishing and all scored big.

Day 27: Free day on Homer Spit, at leisure.

Day 28: Drove 181 miles from Homer to **Seward,** parked on beach in city-run campground.

Day 29: Were treated to boat tour of the **Resurrection Bay** by the tour company. Visited the earthquake museum and historic Seward.

Day 30: At leisure in Seward.

Day 31: Drove 170 miles from Seward to **Palmer** with a side trip to Anchorage supermarkets. Checked into nice campground with all hookups. Had potluck supper in campground.

Day 32: Drove 267 miles from Palmer to **Valdez,** through very scenic country, alongside the Alyeska pipeline for much of the way—good chance for photographs.

Day 33: Were treated to eight-hour cruise to **Columbia Glacier** and to dinner at **Glacier Island.** Wonderful day.

Day 34: Free day in Valdez. Watched spawning salmon close up in a stream entering city. Saw black bears in campground, not the one we were staying in.

Day 35: Drove 259 miles from Valdez to **Tok.**

Day 36: Now we're heading for home. Drove 247 miles from Tok to **Cottonwood Camp,** near magnificent **Kluane Lake** in the Yukon Territory.

Day 37: Drove 395 miles from Kluane Lake to **Whitehorse, Yukon Territory.**

Day 38: At leisure in Whitehorse. Had an excellent sit-down dinner, compliments of the tour company.

Day 39: Drove 120 miles from Whitehorse to **Skagway, Alaska.** Here it was possible to leave the caravan and go home by boat.

Day 40: At leisure in Skagway, spent the day exploring. Great scenery.

Day 41: Drove 151 miles from Skagway, after watching bald eagles, to **Rancheria, Yukon Territory,** for the night.

Day 42: Drove 375 miles of scenic gravel road from Rancheria, Yukon, to **Tagotta Lake, B.C.**

Day 43: Drove 186 miles from Tagotta Lake to **Stewart, B.C.** Arrived in steady rain and watched numerous black bears feeding on spawning salmon. Great pictures!

Day 44: Drove 212 miles from Stewart to **Smithers, B.C.**

Day 45: Drove 235 miles from Smithers to **Prince George, B.C.,** where our tour ended with a farewell dinner hosted by the tour company.

Day 46: On our own; only 800 miles to Lewiston, Idaho, if that interests you.

This was a forty-six-day caravan that included many extras, like catered meals, Frantic Follies, "mellerdrammers" and entry fees. That made it much more expensive than it would have been with a "bare bones" tour. But the social life of a caravan is worth a lot. On the other hand, when traveling alone you can stay an extra day when the spirit moves you, or leave early if the destination doesn't interest you. Traveling alone is safe on this run, and there are many roadside parks where you can camp free. Also, there are a couple of dozen good grayling streams just aching to be fished—and you can enjoy a lot more of that kind of recreation when you're alone.

Alone or in a caravan, a trip to Alaska can be the RV high point of a lifetime. Don't miss it!

There are three publications that will greatly add to your enjoyment of a driving trip to Alaska:

1. Dalby, Ron. *The Alaska Highway: An Insider's Guide,* Revised Edition. Golden, Colorado: Fulcrum Publishing, 1994.

2. Dalby, Ron. *The Alaska Guide.* Golden, Colorado: Fulcrum Publishing, 1994.

3. *The Milepost.* This has been the bible of far north travel since 1949. A priceless guide for motor travelers to Alaska, it is updated annually. Most bookstores can order it for you if they don't have it in stock.

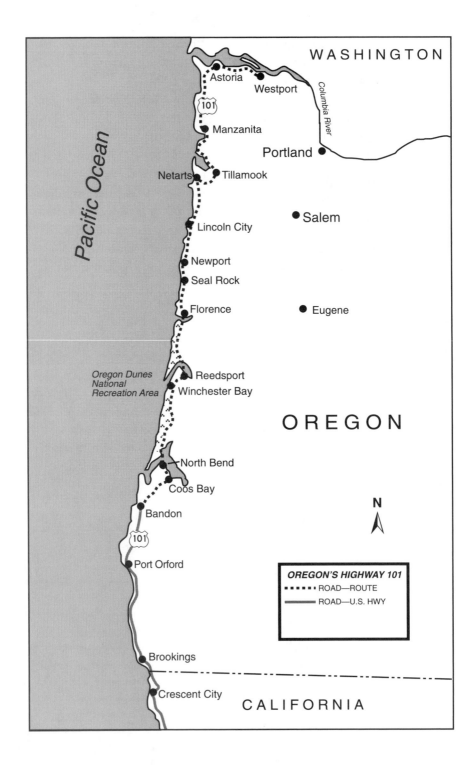

WASHINGTON

Astoria

Westport

Columbia River

(101)

Manzanita

Portland

Netarts • Tillamook

Salem

Lincoln City

Newport

Seal Rock

Florence

Eugene

Pacific Ocean

Oregon Dunes
National
Recreation Area

Reedsport

Winchester Bay

OREGON

North Bend

Coos Bay

Bandon

(101)

N

Port Orford

OREGON'S HIGHWAY 101
•••••• ROAD—ROUTE
━━━ ROAD—U.S. HWY

Brookings

Crescent City   CALIFORNIA

3
Oregon's Coastal Highway 101

Most "coastal" highways run so far off of the coast that you can't see the ocean. But Oregon's Highway 101 actually *is* a coastal highway—you can see the ocean most of the time, and you'll see beautiful scenery all of the time.

This road leads you to the world's smallest harbor, to plants that eat insects, to sea lion caves, to the continent's best ice cream, to a village where they still launch dories through the surf, to quaint little fishing villages—and to a fishing river where you throw back fish that are more than 6 feet long!

The state of Oregon wisely preempted all 400 miles of its coastline,

preserving this idyllic Eden in public ownership. Then they strung a chain of public parks along this highway, to make sure that you and I could enjoy a wonderful RV trip there. Not all of these parks allow camping but many do. You can get a listing of state parks and the facilities they provide by writing to the Oregon State Parks Department, 1115 Commercial Street N.E., Salem, OR 97310-1001, (503) 378-6305.

If you intend to stay in the excellent state parks, make reservations well ahead of time by calling 1-800-452-5687. There is a $6 nonrefundable reservation fee, and you must also pay for the first night of camping upfront. The total cost, including the reservation fee, is $17–$26, depending on the campground. Oregon's state parks are very popular and are almost always full in July and August.

I don't think there is another road in America that can boast of so many attractions. Let's take a quick look.

Naturally, you can drive 101 from south to north, but it's really better to go from north to south, because this puts you closer to the ocean. Also, most of the attractions are on the west side and right turns are easier than left turns.

Starting where 101 enters Oregon from Washington, look for the turnoff to the small town of **Warrenton**. There you can take a fishing boat out into the mighty **Columbia River**. The knowledgeable skipper picks out the best spot—using landmarks you can't even see—and drops the anchor. "Get 'em over," he calls, and you drop a heavy sinker into the rushing tide. That sinker carries a big chunk of bait to attract the primitive fish known as sturgeon. These armor-plated throwbacks to the age of the dinosaurs are bottom feeders. They use a "vacuum cleaner" type of mouth to suck up their food. When they swallow your bait with the hook hidden in it, you'll feel the

fish turn to leave with his meal, and then you sock the hook to him. They are very strong fish, and they fight with stamina.

If your sturgeon is less than 3 feet long, you can't legally keep it; you must put it back so it has a chance to grow up. If the sturgeon is more than 6 feet long, you have to release it because these monsters are the important breeders needed to reproduce and replenish the stock. Sturgeon come in two species—the white and the green—and it's my impression that although the green is not really good to eat, the white is delicious. Sturgeon can also be made into wonderful fish chowder.

The charter operation that we recommend is the 50-foot *Ruby Sea,* operated by **Charlton Deep Sea Charters,** P.O. Box 637, Warrenton, OR 97146, (503) 861-2429. The owner, Captain Mark Charlton, has 20 years' experience. The boat leaves at either 5:30 A.M. or 6:30 A.M. and returns in 8–10 hours. The cost is $65 per angler for sturgeon and salmon fishing and $80 per angler for bottom fishing. Pack a lunch and wear warm clothing, as the breeze off the Columbia can be very cool in the early morning.

It should be mentioned that the daily limit is two sturgeon per angler, but when you remember that the legal fish are about 4 feet long, two are enough.

While in the Warrenton area, you should explore the **Fort Clatsop National Monument,** located on Business 101 south of **Astoria.** Here Lewis and Clark spent the winter after their historic trek from the Mississippi River to the Pacific Ocean. Here they spent the winter, writing and revising their historic journals. For further information write to the Superintendent of Fort Clatsop, Route 3, Box 604-FC, Astoria, OR 97103, (503) 861-2471.

Next stop should be **Ecola State Park.** You can obtain information for the park by calling the Cannon Beach information center, (503) 436-2623. It's shown on your state highway map and is easy to find. After you leave the main highway and start the 2-mile approach to this beautiful park, you may feel that you've made a mistake as the road becomes a tunnel through the dense foliage. My CB antenna struck trees constantly, but no damage was done and the route is perfectly safe. There's a large parking lot with ample room for RVs. Here the camera bug can film some of the most beautiful seascapes on this continent and the spectacle of myriad sea birds on the offshore rocks, which are part of the national wildlife refuge system. While exploring Ecola and vicinity, we camped at **Fort Stevens State Park,** which offers 213 sites

Many side roads in coastal Oregon go right to the scenic seashore.

with full hookups and 130 with electrical hookups. The park is located 10 miles west of Astoria off of US 101; the phone number is (503) 861-1671.

Before heading south on Highway 101, you should stop at the **End of the Trail Monument,** and try to imagine what the first explorers felt when they completed the trip across the western half of the United States and finally came to the shores of the Pacific.

Next stop is **Garibaldi,** a lovely little fishing village where charters are available to take you offshore for salmon in season and to onshore bottom fishing good in all seasons. On our first trip to Garibaldi, we went fishing with Captain Doug Brown and had excellent catches of black rockfish, lingcod and cabezone. I remember a special treat—Captain Brown set out eight crab traps on the way out and picked them up on the return trip. He and his wife, Peggy, cooked the delicious Dungeness crabs when we returned and shared them with all of us anglers. Wonderful. One word of caution is in order; the seas off this coast can be boisterous. If you suffer from seasickness, better beware of this offshore fishing. You can call the *Siggi-G Ocean Charters* in Garibaldi at (503) 322-3285.

The **Garibaldi Marina**, at 302 Mooring Basin Road, Garibaldi, OR 97118, (503) 322-3312, is a good source for information on fishing, clamming and crabbing. They have everything you'll need to rent to enjoy the seafood-gathering possibilities of this second oldest of Oregon port cities.

While in this area, look into the **Fun Run Excursion Train,** which makes a 28-mile run through incomparable scenery every Saturday and Sunday from May 22 through October 11, including a stop for wine tasting at a historic vineyard and winery.

Garibaldi offers some excellent restaurants for your dining pleasure. We enjoyed the Old Mill Restaurant and the Trollers.

While in the Garibaldi vicinity we camped at **Bay City RV Park,** at milepost 61.5 on Highway 101, (503) 377-2124. This camp features 60-foot pull throughs, full hookups, cable TV, a laundry and a small restaurant.

Miami Cove RV Park, 503 East Garibaldi Avenue, Garibaldi, OR 97118, (503) 322-3300, offers only 14 spaces, but they are good ones. This park is on 101 about half a mile from downtown Garibaldi.

Our next stop is **Pacific City,** where we used **Don Johnson's Cape Kiwanda Trailer Park** as our headquarters to enjoy another stretch of magical Highway 101. There are 130 campsites there within sight and sound of the surf. We strolled the lonely beach for hours and watched daring fishermen singlehandedly launch wooden dories directly into the surf. We also visited the **Tillamook Cheese Factory,** (503) 842-4481. Don't smile at the idea of visiting a lowly cheese factory, for this is one of the three most frequently visited spots in all of Oregon. The greatest attraction here is the delicious ice cream in dozens of savory flavors. I've returned often for another ice cream cone, delicious and generous in size.

The parking lot easily accommodates even the largest of RVs. Self-guided tours explain the history of this creamery and allow you the opportunity to see cheeses being made. The gift shop offers many cheeses and mementos. We especially liked the cheese with jalapeño peppers in it.

Speaking of cheese, better visit the nearby **Blue Heron Cheese Factory,**

(503) 842-8281, for more exotic cheeses and sausages.

The **Tillamook Chamber of Commerce** is located south of the Tillamook Cheese Factory; in fact, they use the same parking lot. This is an excellent source of information about camping opportunities in the area. Look for their camping guide on the pamphlet rack. Not only does it list the campgrounds, but is unusual in that it lists campground fees. Also ask for their excellent publication on clamming and crabbing in Tillamook. Even if you're not interested in actually digging up a delicious meal of tasty clams, you'll find this pamphlet informative and educational. Can you tell the difference between razor clams, quahogs, blue clams, cockle clams and littleneck clams?

On other trips we've stayed at **Pleasant Valley RV Park located about** 7 miles south of Tillamook, right on Highway 101. The cost for two people is $19.50 for full hookups and $14 for tent sites. For three or more persons, there is an additional charge of $2 per person. Their phone number is (503) 842-4779.

You might also want to visit the **World War II Blimp Hangar and Museum** just south of Tillamook, or visit **Munson Creek Falls,** which claims to be the highest waterfall on the coast.

We drove the scenic **Three Capes Highway loop,** which leaves 101 and returns to it. On this short but beautiful drive, you'll view sand dunes ten stories tall, deep-shaded forests and secluded coves—all in the one day's drive. On this drive, be sure to visit the **Whiskey Creek Fish Hatchery,** which is a cooperative facility operated by unpaid volunteer sportsmen. If you're the adventurous type, you can take a fishing trip that starts with launching a flat-bottomed, high-ended skiff through the surf near photogenic Haystack Rock—with you in it. It's exciting and a pleasure to watch the expert work of the surf man who holds your destiny in his hands. These surf boats get you out to some excellent salmon fishing in the right season and to good bottom fishing all year long.

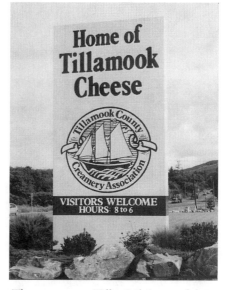

The creamery at Tillamook is one of the three most visited places in all of Oregon.

When returning, they ride an incoming wave to a sliding stop on the wet sand!

We spent two days at **Lincoln City**, enjoying the 7 miles of beaches and the seafood restaurants. Trailer parks and campgrounds are available everywhere in the vicinity of Lincoln City, which appears to live by the tourist trade.

Just to say you've seen it, visit the world's shortest river: the "**D**" **River** flows only 120 feet from its source in Devils Lake to its end in the Pacific Ocean. At the south end of town, you'll find exceptional bird-watching and seal watching in Siletz Bay.

Our next stop was at **Depoe Bay**, called the world's smallest harbor. Here the wild surf has succeeded in punching a hole through the rock cliffs. Once through the cliff, the sea has rounded out a lovely little

Ready for the next day's fishing, sport and commercial boats lie at their moorings inside Depoe Bay.

harbor, snug and secure against the wildest of storms.

The entrance to this harbor is so narrow that there is barely room for two boats to pass through abreast. Leaving the harbor in the usual heavy sea, the boats run at full power to give them good steerage way to make the departure. Once clear of the tiny entrance, they head for the sea buoy and then out to begin a day of bird-watching, whale watching, fishing for salmon or for the ever-present bottom fish.

Whale watching is a big thing here especially just after Christmas, but whales are not always in residence offshore of Depoe Bay. These whales, among the largest creatures that ever lived, use migration routes that come close to shore here. Anxious for your dollars, the whale-watching boats will always take you out if you want to go. A better system is to park on a high spot overlooking the ocean and use your binoculars to look for whales. If you see whales spout—"Thar she blows!"—then you go sign up for a whale-watching trip. Getting up close and personal with these mighty behemoths is a thrilling experience. Be sure to bring your camera along, both on whale-watching trips and when exploring the harbor, for this is a very photogenic place.

While exploring Depoe Bay, we stayed at the beautiful (and expensive)

Holiday Park RV Camp, located right on the water's edge a mile or two north of the tiny town of Depoe Bay. The view as the sun sets over the Pacific is almost justification enough for the high price. Do the showers still cost a quarter?

Boat trips for every purpose are available in Depoe Bay. One of the most experienced outfits is TRADEWINDS, telephone is (541) 765-2345. They provide fishing trips of all kinds, coastal scenery cruises, whale-watching trips, sunset cruises and even long-distance trips ... they'll even provide cruises for a "wedding at sea." Most common of their trips is the 5-hour fishing trip that sells for $50 per person, while 12-hour halibut and tuna trips will run $150.

Next comes **Newport,** one of the larger cities along 101. One of its foremost attractions is the **Oregon Coast Aquarium** on the shores of Yaquina Bay. You can see seals, sea lions and otters, tufted puffins and other sea birds and even a giant Pacific octopus—all that is outside. Inside four large exhibit galleries, you'll get a really good look at the Oregon coastline—and its depth. During the summer it's open from 9:00 A.M. to 6:00 P.M. daily. For more information, phone (541) 867-3474. They do charge an entrance fee, but it's well worth it.

Campgrounds in the Newport vicinity include **Beachside State Park,** on 101, 4 miles south of Waldport, which offers 31 sites with electricity, but maximum length of RV is 30 feet. Phone is (541) 563-3220. **Beverly Beach State Park,** on 101, 7 miles north of Newport, has 52 sites with full hookups, including some really long ones. Phone is (541) 265-4560. **Carl G. Washburne State Park,** on 101, is 14 miles north of Florence with 58 full hookup sites. Phone is (541) 547-3416. **Devils Lake State Park,** on 101 in Lincoln City, has 32 full hookup sites. Call (541) 994-2002. **South Beach State Park,** on 101, is 2 miles south of Newport; 254 sites have electricity. Phone is (541) 867-4715. We stayed a couple of days at South Beach State Park and enjoyed every minute of it.

From this headquarters you'll want to visit both **Yaquina Bay Lighthouse** and **Heceta Head Lighthouse.** Yaquina Bay installation has been authentically restored to its 1871 condition.

Our next stop was **Florence,** known as the gateway to the **Oregon Dunes National Recreation Area,** a huge scenic sand pile that stretches along the coast for many miles, inviting travelers to beachcomb, to photograph and to enjoy the tang of the salt air.

Plan to spend more than a day in the 47-mile-long Oregon Dunes, for they are much more than just a big sand pile. This is a place to observe the never-ending battle between the sea and the land, a meeting place of several life zones, a home to many birds and animals and a superb place to photograph tiny chipmunks—unafraid and within camera range. The biggest problem is in getting them to hold still long enough for even an autofocus lens to do its job. These giant dunes border the sea all the way to the north shore of Coos Bay.

Several access points to the dunes provide wooden walkways giving you an elevated view of the big sand dunes. Climbing to the uppermost tier, you'll see the dunes as snow white spaces between coastal dunes and the beginnings of the forest. Hikers far out on the white sands seem to be as small as ants against the immense background. The inexorable advance of the slow-drifting sand threatens to engulf and smother vegetation—and sometimes it wins. Where did all this sand come from? Geologic ages ago, this part of Oregon was under the sea. The sea floor was pushed up into a mountain range. Heavy rains eroded these coastal mountains and rivers carried the resulting sand to the sea. Waves and tidal action moved the sand onto the shore, and the onshore winds did the rest, constantly moving the sand and forcing it farther inland where it wages its battle against the forest.

For an in-depth look at the dunes, take a dune buggy ride. One such ride is offered by **Sand Dunes Frontier and Theme Park** on 101 just 4 miles south of Florence. Half-hour tours cost about $10 for ages 12 and over. You can rent your own four wheeler for $35 per hour after a $100 deposit. Their phone number is (541) 997-3544.

Florence is the "City of Rhododendrons," and during May and June the highways are ablaze with color—the pink and red of rhododendrons, the yellow of Scotch broom, the reds of Indian paintbrush and the whites of myriad daisies. Do-it-yourself clamming or crabbing is productive, or you can buy the succulent seafood at market prices along the highway. Restaurants feature Dungeness crab and prepare it well.

The **Siuslaw Pioneer Museum** at Milepost 192 on Highway 101 South in Florence is worth a short visit to see the Native American and early pioneer artifacts. Their address is P.O. Box 2637, Florence, OR 97439, (541) 997-7884.

Twelve miles north of Florence, on Highway 101, you'll find the famous **Sea Lion Caves.** The admission fee is $6.50 for 16 and older and $4.50 for ages 6–15. You can walk along the edge of a high cliff from which you can look down at the sea lions on the rocks below, enjoying their only rookery on the mainland; all others are on islands. Next you ride a modern elevator 208 feet down through the rocks to the caves that are the safe haven for the sea lions, some of them weighing as much as a ton. The sea has been working on this big cave for millennia, and it is now twelve stories high inside and longer than a football field. There is often enough light to allow you to take pictures here—of the sea lions and the cave itself—but you must use a very fast film, preferably one with an ASA speed of 1000. Because I prefer color slides, I used Kodachrome 200, a 300-millimeter telephoto lens and leaned against a rock wall to steady my camera for the necessarily long exposure. If you have questions about the Sea Lion Caves, you can call (541) 547-3111.

Cape Perpetua Visitor Center, P.O. Box 274, Yachats, OR 97498, is a 2,700-acre scenic area operated by the U.S. Forest Service, featuring such tidal action attractions as the **Devil's Churn.** Cape Perpetua offers 18 miles of interesting hiking trails down to the rocky beach, tide pool exploring and wildlife viewing. The Cape Perpetua overlook is a spectacular spot for photographing the rugged meeting place of sea and rock.

If you're a dedicated fisherman, get a copy of the *Fishing Guide to the Oregon Dunes National Recreation Area,* which details a surprisingly large number of fishing lakes in the dunes, and gives helpful hints about fishing tactics and instructions as to how to reach these waters. And for the fly-fishing fanatic, visit the **Fly-Fishing Museum** at 280 Nopal Street in Florence. It features a beautiful collection of flies and sells everything for the fly-fishing collector. It is open summers from 10 A.M. to 5 P.M.

Florence offers **sternwheel cruises** up the historic **Siuslaw River.** There are morning cruises for wildlife viewing, mid-day Lazy Riverboat parties and romantic evening cruises. Prices range from $15 to $35. Dinner on board is extra of course. For up-to-date information regarding sailing times, telephone (541) 268-4017.

No visit to Florence would be complete without a walking tour of Old Town, with its restored historic buildings and more than sixty-five shops to serve you.

And before you leave Florence, be sure to point your camera at a blood-red sunset over the Pacific, framed by the sand dunes of this magical area.

Leaving Florence, it is but a few minutes drive down to the **Darling-**

ton Wayside where you can park and walk in to see the insect-eating plants we told you about. Cobra lilies, sometimes called "pitcher plants" lure insects into their open tops, close over them and digest them. It's about a 200-yard walk to the spot, and that 200 yards is often guarded by ferocious mosquitoes, so bring along some good insect repellent and use it generously. The plants eat insects, but you don't want to have the insects eat you.

Continuing south on magical 101, you come to **Winchester Bay,** home of **Salmon Harbor.** A charter fleet that operates out of the harbor specializes in short runs to productive salmon waters. A special one-day fishing license is available, and you can have your catch canned locally so that you can take it home for bragging purposes. We ate salmon till it ran out of our ears and consumed it all so we had no need for canning.

Here you can camp right on the dock itself, with no hookups, for a fee of $7 per night. If you don't want to charter a boat and catch your own, you can enjoy excellent seafood meals at the **Seafood Grotto,** at 8th Street and Broadway. Their phone is (541) 271-4250.

You'll probably want to photograph the historic **Umpqua Lighthouse.** Modern electronics has made it obsolete, but it is maintained as a part of the historic heritage and to remind us of the dangers inherent in seafaring off this rocky coast.

Next stop is **Coos Bay,** the most important port in this section of the Pacific coast. We stayed right on the water in **Charleston Harbor,** where we discovered the excellent seafood of the **Portside Restaurant.** Coquille St. Jacques, fresh halibut sauté and a wonderful crab thermidor were among the choices of our party, and we were all pleased with our meals.

Coos Bay features a deep water port where Oregon lumber leaves for Japanese markets. It also offers a healthy charter boat fishery specializing, as always, in salmon. Charter boats are plentiful and many operate from Charleston Harbor just southwest of Coos Bay itself. Rental tackle is available for those who don't carry their own. Two of the charter boat skippers are **Bob's Sport Fishing,** (541) 888-4241, and **Betty Kay Charters,** (541) 888-9021.

Aficionados of lighthouses will find three to visit. **Umpqua Lighthouse** has its own state park north of Coos Bay. This park is also a good location for whale watching from December through May. This is the oldest lighthouse on the Oregon Coast, dating back to 1857. **Cape Arago Lighthouse** was built in 1866. Destroyed by erosion in its original site, the lighthouse was reconstructed in its present location in

1934. **Coquille River Lighthouse** was built in 1886 and served coastal navigators till 1963.

Myrtlewood, a very dense blond hardwood, grows best in this southwestern corner of Oregon, and there are many shops specializing in articles made of this beautiful wood in and near to Coos Bay. To start your investigation, we recommend **The House of Myrtlewood,** P.O. Box 457, Coos Bay, OR 97420. It is right on 101. Here you can watch the entire process, from raw log to finished article.

West Coast Game Park Safari, Route 1, Box 1330, Bandon, OR 97411, telephone (541) 347-3106, is 19 miles south of Coos Bay on 101. Here is a chance to get close to many exotic and native species of animals. Almost all animals on exhibit in this 27-acre park have been hand-raised, which accounts for their being so tame. Bring your camera!

We headquartered at the **Bandon/Port Orford KOA.** This KOA is not located in either Bandon or Port Orford but halfway between at Langlois, Oregon, right on Highway 101. This is a pleasant place, with most sites in deep shade, which helps in August. This KOA offers its own brand of cable TV, piping the programs to the sites from its own satellite disk. Worked well when we were there.

If time dictates, you can end your exciting trip down the road of surprises, Oregon's Coastal Highway 101, right here. If you have time to continue on, several more spots beckon. We'd recommend **Gold Beach,** where you can take a jet boat trip. Later you can explore the cities of **Pistol River** and **Brookings** for further study. No matter how much time you invest, you'll never see all of the attractions of Highway 101, the coastal highway that really is a coastal highway. Take your time to explore in depth, and you'll agree that this is one of the greatest RV trips!

Waterton Glacier
International Peace Park

CANADA

WA

Browning

Kalispell

93

MONTANA

ND

90

OR

Bison Range
Missoula

94

IDAHO

90

Butte

Billings

Bozeman

SD

15

Yellowstone N.P.

90

Bolter Bay

WYOMING

84

Grand
Teton
N.P.

86

287

84

Great
Salt
Lake

80

Rawlins

25

NE

Laramie

Cheyenne

80

80

Salt Lake City

Rocky
Mtn.
N.P.

76

70

Granby

Denver

70

NV

15

UTAH

COLORADO

KAN

25

OK

40

Albuquerque

CA

ARIZONA

NEW MEXICO

ROCKY MOUNTAIN PARKS
•••••• ROAD—ROUTE
——— ROAD—INTERSTATE

N

MEXICO

TEXAS

4

Along the Rockies from Colorado to Montana

Many RVers believe that the most beautiful parts of the United States are those found above 8,500 feet. If you agree, then this trip is for you! We're going to start out just an hour's drive north of Denver, Colorado, and end up within sight of Canada in Glacier National Park.

To make the entire trip and do it right, you'll need about a month, but the beauty of this trip is that you can make it in sections, enjoying as much of the fascinating high country as your vacation schedule will allow, then come back next vacation and pick up where you left off. The beauty and majesty of the Rockies will still be there to thrill you.

Rocky Mountain National Park

Estes Park, Colorado, is the entrance city to **Rocky Mountain National Park.** Turn west off of Interstate 25 onto Highway 34 and drive through the beautiful Big Thompson Canyon to Estes Park, a city that seems to exist only to cater to the 2.6 million visitors that come to the park every year. One thing is certain, you won't be alone very often in this huge mountain playground unless you go hiking—then you'll leave civilization behind rather quickly. Three miles off the road and you have the world to yourself.

The first duty is to locate a campground, because most of them fill up by early afternoon. Two of the park service's campgrounds, **Moraine Park** and **Glacier Basin,** accept reservations but call early. You can make reservations up to eight weeks in advance for these two campgrounds by calling 1-800-365-2267. There are several commercial campgrounds right in Estes Park, and there are many along the river on your way in. I'd suggest calling ahead for reservations during the summer months.

You might want to try:

Estes Park Campground, P.O. Box 247, Allenspark, CO 80510, (970) 586-4188; 12 RV spaces.
Mary's Lake Campground, P.O. Box 2514, Estes Park, CO 80517, (970) 586-4411; 110 RV spaces.
National Park Resort Campground, 3501 Fall River Road, Estes Park, CO 80517, (970) 586-4563; 100 RV spaces.
Yogi Bear's Jellystone Park of Estes, 5495 U.S. Highway 36, Estes Park, CO 80517, (970) 586-4230; 60 RV spaces.
Spruce Lake RV Park, P.O. Box 2497, Estes Park, CO 80517, (970) 586-2889; 1,100 RV spaces.

There is an excellent **KOA Campground** right on Highway 34 at the west edge of Estes Park, 2051 Big Thompson Avenue, Estes Park, CO 80517, (970) 586-2888.

Estes Park is a good headquarters city and offers everything you might need as you enjoy the 414 square miles of Rocky Mountain National Park. Colorado contains much of the really high country in the United States, so it shouldn't surprise you that seventy-six mountain peaks here reach the 12,000-foot mark.

We've listed a few of the campgrounds, and you shouldn't venture into the park without having made your reservation. Also, get out your Golden Age Passport, if you have one. Currently, anyone who is sixty-two or older can purchase the Golden Age Passport for a one-time fee of $10. The passport allows the bearer to enter federal parks for free and to receive 50 percent off facilities within the park. If you're too young to qualify for the Golden Age Passport, it will cost you $5 per vehicle every time you enter.

Once you're in the park, you should head directly for the visitors' center to get yourself oriented with the park roads and with its main attractions. **Park Visitor Center and Park Headquarters** is located just west of Estes Park. If you're coming from the west on Highway 34, visit the **Kewuneeche Visitor Center** at the park entrance. The best place to learn more about the park is **Moraine Park Museum** 2 $^1/_2$ miles southwest of the headquarters—excellent exhibits here. There is also the brand new **Lily Lake Visitor Center** on Highway 7, 8 miles south of Estes Park.

Rocky Mountain National Park offers many things to many people—hiking on more than 350 miles of trails, bird-watching, big game watching, camping, fishing, rock climbing, horseback rides, photography, study of alpine environments and bicycling are just a few of the activities here. Its greatest attraction is also the most accessible—**Trail Ridge Road,** the magnificent highway that takes you halfway to the stars as it winds and twists its way to the top of the park and the **Alpine Visitor Center.** The road was planned to handle a lot of visitors with many turnouts and parking areas. Some of these point the way to short walks to another point where an even more majestic scene is available for your camera and for your eyes.

Please take your time and allow the beauty of the park to soak in—don't rush through it. There is no prize for getting to the other end quickly—take your time and you'll see the most beautiful part of this beautiful state of Colorado.

Weather is always a concern in the high country. The first permanent settler was Joel Estes and his wife, who homesteaded in what is now Estes Park in 1860. Estes intended to ranch cattle, but the winters proved too much for the cattle, and he gave up the fight after six years. I'm tempted to advise you to visit Rocky Mountain National Park after Labor Day, when the crowds are gone and the fall foliage is ablaze with color. But snow can fall anytime after the first of September, causing temporary road closures. Shortly after Thanksgiving the snowplows give up and the vital road link between Estes Park and Grand Lake is left to the drifts until June.

Wet weather can blow in within minutes on Trail Ridge Road, and this means that you should carry warm clothing at all times. Even in early August, the breeze atop Trail Ridge can feel like it just came off the glacier's ice (and maybe it did).

Parking space for large RVs is provided on Trail Ridge Road.

Summer heat can be brutal at high elevations with so little to screen out the sun's rays. If you hike, carry lots of water and wear sound hiking shoes.

After you've traversed Trail Ridge slowly in both directions, your next visit should be to **Bear Lake.** Please note that you can save gas by parking at the trail head and riding the free shuttle bus that will take you to Bear Lake itself. Here, I hope you'll take a leisurely stroll completely around the lake—it isn't very big, and most of the walk is in the shade.

Bring lots of color film, for this roof of the world park is incredibly scenic. "You can take a calendar picture anywhere you point the camera," one RVer remarked to me.

Have your camera ready at all times, for several thousand elk make their home in the park—we saw elk cows at ranges of less than 20 feet, but they were in deep stands of timber. Larger groups of up to twenty-five animals were seen at great distances as they fed in the open meadows below the scenic overlooks on Trail Ridge Road. Moose and black bear reside in the park but are seldom seen from the roads. Colorado's emblem, the majestic bighorn sheep, is increasing in numbers; the best place to see them is in **Horseshoe Park.** My favorite wildlife, however, are the hoary marmots and the golden-mantled ground squirrels and the omnipresent Clark's nutcrackers, who cadge food from visitors at every pullout, despite park regulations forbidding artificial feeding.

Here are the phone numbers you'll need to learn more about the park:

Park Headquarters: (970) 586-1206
Backcountry information, for backpacking and hiking info: (970) 586-1242
Reservations for the two park campgrounds that will accept advance reservations: 1-800-365-2267
Estes Park Chamber of Commerce: 1-800-44-ESTES
Grand Lake Chamber of Commerce: (970) 627-3402
State Patrol road conditions: (303) 639-1111

Tame wildlife in Rocky Mountain National Park includes the golden-mantled ground squirrel.

Grand Teton National Park

From the highest spots in Rocky Mountain National Park you can see Wyoming, and we now head for the northeast corner of that lovely state to the most photogenic of all national parks, **Grand Teton.**

In Grand Teton, it seems as though every mountain has its own reflecting basin to mirror its loveliness. The rugged crags of **Grand Teton National Park** were formed by gigantic upheavals of the earth as one tectonic plate ground its way into and under another plate. Then the 3,000-foot thick glaciers of the Ice Age covered the upthrust mountains, and as the glaciers moved inexorably onward, they ground and sliced the rugged mountains into the magnificent range we see today. As the glaciers melted and retreated, the rushing torrents of water carved the mountains even more. Glaciers can still be seen doing their work high on the slopes of **Mount Owens, Grand Teton Mountain** and the **Teewinot Range,** all visible from either of the two main roads that run north and south through the park.

But before you start to enjoy the beauty of Grand Teton, it's wise to pick a campground. Some of the five camps operated by the National Park Service (NPS) fill up as early as 8:00 A.M. during the summer. These campsites charge $8 per night. Let's skip **Jenny Lake Campground** be-

In one of the most photogenic of all national parks, the Grand Teton Mountains tower above everything.

cause it is for tenters only. That leaves **Signal Mountain Campground** with 86 spaces, dump station and drinking water but no hookups; **Colter Bay Campground** with 350 spaces, dump station and drinking water but no hookups; **Lizard Creek** with 62 sites, no dumping station and no hookups; and **Gros Ventre** with 360 sites, dump station but no utility hookups. Reservations are not accepted; all these campgrounds are on a first-come, first-serve basis.

In addition to the NPS campgrounds, there are two huge concessionaire-operated campgrounds—

Colter Bay Village, which has 1,122 sites with full hookups. Advance reservations are accepted; write to Grand Teton Lodge Company, P.O. Box 240, Moran, WY 83013, or call (307) 733-2811. The second concession campground is the **Flagg Ranch,** which has 100 sites with full hookups. Advance reservations also accepted. Write to Flagg Ranch, P.O. Box 187, Moran, WY 83013, or call (307) 543-2861. After June 1, call (307) 543-2364.

Some RVers may desire to stay outside the park in commercial campgrounds. One option on Highway 287 is the **Grand Teton Park RV Resort,** 1-800-563-6469. There are good **KOA campgrounds** just outside of **Jackson, Wyoming,** on the road to **Teton Village,** (307) 733-5354, and another at **South Jackson,** on Highway 191, (307) 733-7078. Other campgrounds are available right in the town of Jackson. Contact the Chamber of Commerce in Jackson at (307) 733-3316 for further information. Jackson is a good source of camping supplies, groceries and anything you might need to make your trip a success.

Think of the road system of Grand Teton as being a circle flattened east to west, with its northern terminus at the dam that formed Jackson Lake and its southern terminus at the **Moose Visitor Center,** which is the park headquarters. If you want to move fast—within speed limits, of course—take the eastern side of the circle. If you have lots of time and want to see more wildlife, take the western side of the circle, which goes in to the shores of **Jenny Lake.** Excellent turnouts are provided at all scenic viewpoints. You can see everything of note from this circle drive—with one exception. I strongly recommend that you take the turnoff south of the Signal Mountain Campground, the turnoff that leads to the top of **Signal Mountain.** The summit affords a view of the park you can't get anywhere else. Although the road is narrow and winding, it is hard-surfaced and kept in good condition. Even the largest motor homes can handle its turns. Trailers are prohibited, of course, but if you're traveling by trailer you'll leave it in the campground anyway. The very best photo opportunity on this drive is halfway down on the return trip, where there's a small turnoff with a spectacular view of Jackson Lake. Put a pine tree at each edge of the picture to frame it and add depth, and you've got a spectacular shot.

Another "not to be missed" photograph is available from the **Oxbow Bend** turnout at the north end, where the snow-mantled mountains are reflected in the water—beautiful!

When you've finally gotten accustomed to the sheer beauty of the park, then what is there to do? Plenty! Guided lake-fishing trips are available from Colter Bay Village, where you have a chance to catch lake trout up to 50 pounds, native cutthroat trout and some lunker brown trout. Guided float-trip fishing is also available on the river below **Jackson Dam**. Scenic cruises on the big lake are available throughout the day. For information and for trip reservations, call (307) 543-2811 or, if you're calling from Jackson, (307) 543-2811.

A different kind of river raft float trip is offered by **Barker-Ewing Scenic Tours,** P.O. Box 100, Moose, WY 83012. Their emphasis is on sightseeing, and their rafts are designed with the Snake River in mind. For information and reservations, call 1-800-365-1800. If calling locally, dial (307) 733-1800. These river-raft trips are safe enough for Aunt Minnie but exciting enough for anyone. You'll get a different view of the country, believe me!

Horseback trail rides of all sorts are available, call or just ask at any one of the visitor centers.

A visit to the **Jackson National Fish Hatchery,** just north of the city of Jackson on Highway 191 will show you thousands of young trout growing strong in the protected raceways until they're big enough to be released into the streams and lakes of this lovely land.

About 3,000 elk summer in the park itself and go south to the **National Elk Refuge** to spend the winter. During fall migration into the park, herds of as many as 250 elk can be seen. This park is unusual in that carefully regulated hunting of elk is permitted to keep the elk population within the carrying capacity of the park (in other words, to keep the elk from becoming so numerous that they can't find enough food).

Moose are fairly common within Grand Teton, and you'll be most apt to see them if you watch the shallow water areas, especially at Oxbow Bend turnoff. They feed on water plants and are quite a sight when they put their entire head under water to graze on submerged vegetation. Mule deer may be encountered almost everywhere in the park, especially at sunrise and sunset. Pronghorn antelope are found on the sagebrush flats but not in great numbers. The bighorn sheep is a creature of the high mountain canyons and is seldom seen, except by hikers. You'll also see buffalo (bison) along **Teton Park Road,** and there are several captive herds in the vicinity.

Yellowstone National Park

Our next stop is **Yellowstone,** the first and foremost of the world's national parks. Half an hour's drive north of Grand Teton, you enter the fantastic world of Yellowstone. Here is a land where two major rivers are born, where the **Yellowstone River** dives over the tremendous falls at **Artist Point** and **Inspiration Point,** where you can catch a trout in a tributary of the Missouri River and cook it in a nearby stream heated by geothermal action. This is "Colter's Hell," a land of geysers, mud fountains and steaming holes in the earth. This is the park that features the **Old Faithful Geyser** and 100 smaller geysers that serve as release valves for the pressures built up far beneath the surface of the earth. This is the land where black bears used to stop traffic. Since the enlightened policy of the National Park Service has moved the black bear back away from the roads and campgrounds, we now have bison jams and elk jams and even an occasional moose jam.

Old Faithful, right on time with its eruption, Yellowstone National Park.

Yellowstone entertains several million visitors every summer yet is so vast that you can go hiking on trails leading to solitude, peace and quiet, far from the madding throng of automobiles. Yellowstone offers excellent fishing on the big lake and along the countless small streams that carry the snowmelt down from the high country. Like Grand Teton, it's a photographer's dream, especially for the wildlife photographer. Yellowstone does shelter grizzly bears, which has a "bearing" on which trails to hike, but it does not have grizzlies to the extent that Glacier National Park does.

Everything about Yellowstone is big, including the number of NPS-operated campgrounds—eleven campgrounds with a total of 1,853 individual sites—but in the summer months every campsite is occupied every single night.

Reservations are not accepted at ten of these campgrounds. Only **Bridge Bay** takes advance reservations but charges $2 per night more than the other campgrounds. For advance reservations, telephone 1-800-365-2267. It's a good idea to have alternate dates in mind when calling, for chances are very great that you won't get your first choice. All NPS campgrounds provide water, but none have full hookups. Dump stations are provided at the four largest campgrounds.

It is possible to find hookups in the park. The **RV Trailer Park** near **Fishing Bridge** offers full hookups for $18 per day. Strangely enough, this campground is restricted to "hard-sided" RVs only, no tents or tent trailers are permitted. For information or reservations call (307) 344-7311 or write to TW Services, Inc., Yellowstone National Park, WY 82190.

There are many campgrounds in **West Yellowstone** (in the town, Montana and just outside the park boundary), along the **John D. Rockefeller Memorial Freeway,** which connects Yellowstone and Grand Teton National Parks, and especially at the **Flagg Ranch,** which was mentioned under Grand Teton.

How best to see this wonderland? There are six informational leaflets—named for the six areas of the park: Norris Geyser Basin, Mammoth Hot Springs, Mud Volcano, Fountain Paint Pot, Upper Geyser and Canyon. These are for sale for 25¢ each at all visitor centers within the park. Each one is a good investment, and each one tells you which things to see and contains a sketch map to help you find your way. For example, the leaflet on the Grand Canyon of the Yellowstone gives you directions to Artist Point and Inspiration Point—two of the most often photographed scenes in the world. It also tells you much about the geology of the canyon and gives directions to the visitor center, riding stables and the many hiking trails. Plan on slow travel—that way, you won't be disappointed.

You'll be handed an excellent map of Yellowstone when you enter the park. Yes, the Golden Age Passport is honored here. That map will probably remain unfolded and ready for use at all times. But it's best if someone other than the driver does the map reading. The roads in the park are in poor condition due to overuse and lack of maintenance funds. You may disagree, but here are my suggestions as to what is most interesting.

1. **Old Faithful Geyser** and the associated geysers and geothermal attractions of **Biscuit Basin** and **Black Sand Basin. Grand Geyser** and **Crested Pool** are really more interesting than the most famous geyser—Old Faithful. I strongly recommend getting out of your car and walking some of the geyser trails.

2. The **Grand Canyon of the Yellowstone,** especially Artist and Inspiration Points. You have to walk short distances to reach these spots, but the walk is well rewarded. While driving this area, keep a lookout for bison herds and the occasional moose.

3. **Firehole Lake Drive** takes you to **Great Fountain Geyser,** which I have seen erupt to a height of almost 200 feet, and to many other geyser attractions all within short walks of your parked RV. Also please visit the **Fountain Paint Pot** with its fantastic assortment of colors formed by algae and bacteria and mineral deposits from deep within the earth. This area is a good place to study the effects of the 1959 earthquake, which altered the volcanic-geyser scene considerably. Stay on boardwalks where provided—going exploring could cause you to drop through a thin crust into boiling water, which could spoil more than your day.

4. The **Mud Volcanoes,** which really are volcanoes in action. Here it is doubly dangerous to leave the boardwalks. Don't take chances; you can see everything from the boardwalks. Don't let the unpleasant smell of sulfur compounds deter you—this area is well worth an in-depth look.

5. When you enter from the north side of the park, you're almost in the **Mammoth Hot Springs** area. Stop at the **Albright Visitor Center** first, and then drive both the upper and lower terrace roads to see how rain and snow supply the water and the underground furnace provides the heat to produce the everchanging world of travertines and algal blooms, fantastic colors and clear blue waters. Minerals from within the earth are dissolved, carried to the surface by hot water and then, as the water evaporates, the minerals remain to form the beautiful terraced springs you see here.

6. The **Norris Geyser Basin** and the **Norris Overlook Museum** are worthy of a visit. This is an excellent place to learn about the history of the park, especially its early days when it was operated by the U.S. Army. A very different collection of active geysers are displayed to the visitor who takes the time to hike the boardwalks.

7. The wildlife is one of the greatest attractions, but you can't program or schedule their appearances. The best places to see bison are in the neighborhood of the road north from **Fishing Bridge** (which is now closed to fishing) to **Canyon Village.** This is an especially good area for the bison photographer, as it is open

country and the bison are often found very near the road.

In my experience, the best place to see elk is near the west entrance, in open meadows along the **Madison River.**

Moose? Near **Lewis Lake** at the south end of the park, and on the brushy flats along the Yellowstone River from Fishing Bridge to the Mud Volcano area are likely spots—but moose may be found wherever there is a combination of water and brushy areas. Do *not* approach any large wild animals—ever! Even the placid-looking, cud-chewing bison is very unpredictable, and visitors have been tossed, gored and trampled. Let them have their space, for your own safety. This is also excellent advice when viewing moose and bears, either black or grizzly. Day hikes are very popular here and each visitor center can provide the latest information about many hikes. There is a NPS publication that describes twenty of these hikes, ranging from easy to fairly strenuous.

Backpacking is another, very different activity. It is mandatory that you check in with the ranger stations before going on any overnight hike in the 2.2 million acres of the park. If you're moving into the backcountry, you'll want to make plenty of noise so as not to surprise

a grizzly. I watched a trio of young women coming in from a four-day backpacking hike. I asked one of them, who carried a tinkling bell affixed to her pack, "Doesn't that bell noise get monotonous?" She replied, "Not when you consider the alternative!"

There's never a dull moment in this gigantic wonderland. Every possible outdoor activity except hunting is allowed here: horseback rides, guided fishing, hiking, backcountry exploring, photography or just plain marveling at nature's wonders. Yellowstone is the first national park, the biggest in the Lower 48 and perhaps the most spectacular destination of any RV trip.

National Bison Range

It's a long way west of Yellowstone to Missoula, Montana, but when you consider that it's almost all on the wide, sweeping curves of divided Interstate 94, it doesn't seem so far. Both **Bozeman** and **Missoula** are well supplied with campgrounds and stores offering anything you might need. Our next stop is not a national park, but rather a National Wildlife Refuge, operated by the U.S. Fish and Wildlife Service, another branch of the Department of the Interior. Leaving Missoula on Interstate 90 westbound, watch for the turnoff onto Highway 93 heading north to **Glacier National Park.**

This bull ignored my motor coach on the National Bison Range.

Keep your eyes peeled for the signs that guide you off 93 onto the blacktopped road leading to the **National Bison Range.** You can park your trailer in their big parking lot or, if you're towing a motor car behind your coach, leave the motor coach behind and travel by car. If you're driving a coach without towed vehicle, not to worry. You can handle the 19-mile gravel road that leads to the top of **Red Sleep Mountain Drive** and back down the hairpin turns of the descent.

But before you go anywhere, spend an hour or so in the **visitors' center** to give yourself an idea of the lay of the land and to learn about the history of the bison—once numbered in the hundreds of millions, then almost exterminated and now flourishing again in a number of sanctuaries such as this. Now you're ready to begin.

Within the first few miles of the one-way drive, you'll gain almost 1,000 feet in elevation and enjoy some spectacular views of the **Flathead Valley** far below. You'll see plenty of bison—individuals, small groups and perhaps even herds of three hundred to four hundred. Follow instructions, and do not leave your vehicle to take pictures. Bison are unpredictable. They're also huge and surprisingly fast. Stay in or near your vehicle and the bison will graze unconcernedly right around you—so close you can hear their bellies rumble. This is the best place in the world to photograph bison at close range and in natural surroundings. If you're lucky, you'll also see mule deer on this part of the ascent.

When you reach the higher stretches of the road, you'll drive through a forested area—right on the very highest point of the ridge. This is a good place to watch out for bighorn sheep, especially if the day is very hot and the sheep are looking for a cooling breeze.

After you break out of the forested portion, you'll come to the downhill section of the road, and a wonderful view stretches out before you—a view that includes the six or seven hairpin turns waiting for you on the road below. Check your brakes and shift to a lower gear to retard your descent without burning up your brakes. There's not much to look at on the way down, and that's a good thing as you'll be busy watching the road and maneuvering the hairpin turns. Once down near the bottom, you'll come to the well-named **Antelope Ridge;** antelope will usually be in sight all along this side of the refuge. While the bucks stay aloof, the does and young antelope are trusting enough to come within 10 feet of your vehicle, allowing for good photographs.

I'd advise you to plan on an hour for the **visitors' center** and slightly more than two and a half hours for the driving part of your tour of the National Bison Range—easily accomplished in half a day. Picnicking is allowed in the refuge, but not camping. However, the visitors' center will give you a list of twenty campgrounds within 60 miles of the Bison Range. There's free camping right next to the **Senior Citizens' Center** in **Charlo, Montana,** about 8 miles north of the refuge on the way to the last stop on our tour of Glacier National Park. The road will take you along the beautiful shores of **Flathead Lake.** Campground facilities are available in many places on the lake front.

Glacier National Park

In the early days, prior to 1910, only the very rich could see a part of what is now Glacier National Park. They rode the luxurious cars of the Great Northern Railroad and stayed in the sumptuous lodges operated by that same railroad. Now you can see much more than they ever saw, and do it from the comfort of your RV.

Today most of this vast wonderland is administered as a wilderness area and that is its greatest attraction to me. The second greatest attraction is diametrically opposed to the whole idea of wilderness—the magnificent **Going to the Sun Highway** that crosses the very middle of the park, from **St. Mary.** I think this is the most beautiful road in the world. That's a big statement, but after you've driven it I think you'll agree. It was built in the first half of the 1930s and is still regarded as an engineering miracle. The road has seen many changes, the most important being the asphalt surfacing completed in 1957. According to National Park Service literature, you should allow two and a half to three hours to make the drive from **West Glacier,** over the top, to St. Mary on the east end. Don't you believe it! Plan on five to seven hours, with stops at each and every turnout to enjoy the spectacular vistas, and at least an hour at the visitors' center atop **Logan Pass.**

Roads are in better condition and easier on the driver than the roads in Yellowstone, and traffic isn't quite as heavy. However, it's still a good idea to line up your camp-

In late June, snow still lingers in Glacier National Park, especially at the heights reached by Going to the Sun Highway, one of the engineering marvels of the entire parks system.

ground before entering the park. **Kalispell, Montana,** west of the park entrance, has many campgrounds, and there are excellent campgrounds at West Glacier near the park entrance. My personal favorite is the big **KOA at West Glacier, (406) 387-5341.** It's 2 $^1/_2$ miles west of the park entrance, then 1 mile south on a paved road—very quiet and peaceful. Another KOA at the eastern end of the Going to the Sun Road is **KOA St. Mary,** at P.O. Box 1390, St. Mary Route, Browning, MT 59417, (406) 732-4122.

The NPS operates eleven campgrounds on a first-come, first-serve basis. No reservations are accepted in any of these campgrounds. For RV use, the best possibilities are **Avalanche Campground** with 87 sites, but a maximum permitted RV

length of 26 feet; **Apgar,** at the west entrance with 196 sites and a maximum permitted RV length of 35 feet; **Fish Creek** with 80 large RV sites, out of its 180 total; **Many Glacier** with 114 sites and a maximum RV length of 35 feet; and **St. Mary** with 156 sites and a maximum RV length of 30 feet.

So far we've only mentioned Going to the Sun Road, but don't plan on driving your motor coach over that road. I drove a 31-footer over it in years past, but the NPS has set new rules, and you can't drive over the top if you're more than 20 feet long or more than 7 $^1/_2$ feet wide including mirrors.

This means that you can explore the park from West Glacier in to Avalanche Creek campground, but then you must turn around and go back. The best way to see the top of the world here is to park the big coach and drive your towed vehicle on the **Logan Pass Road.** Or park the trailer and use your tow vehicle to the top and back. Or park in Kalispell and rent a car for the drive. Or ride the famous red rubberneck buses that give you a guided tour over and back with stops at all the points of interest and with knowledgeable guide-drivers to point out the wonders. Last time we looked, it cost $47 round-trip and that was a bargain. Or you can ride the shuttle buses, which will take you from one side to the other for $13—but without the informational tour stuff—just plain transportation.

Don't miss the trip over the top, whatever you do!

What else to do?

Drive the edge of **Lake Mc-Donald**; drive U.S. Highway 2, which follows the southern boundary of the park, stopping at **Goat Lick,** a few miles east of **Essex,** and walk to the overlook where you can often see mountain goats licking the mineral-rich soil to get their minerals and vitamins; drive to **Two Medicine Lake** and take the boat tour when you get to the end of the road. But don't plan on taking your motor coach on the shortcut between Two Medicine Lake and Highway 89 en route to St. Mary—the same size restrictions apply here on this short, steep and twisting road as on the Going to the Sun Highway.

Drive the west end of the big highway, from St. Mary along the beautiful lake of the same name to **Sun Point**—that's as far as you can go with the big RV. Drive the beautiful road from **Babb** to **Many Glacier**—best place in the park to see black bears and maybe even a grizzly. Here a word about bears is warranted. Grizzly bears are very dangerous and very unpredictable. Black bears are usually more timid and apt to run away when they get a whiff of humans. Do *not* approach any

bear, at any time, *ever!* When walking through this fantastic scenery, make sure you make enough noise so that you won't surprise a bear. If it knows you're coming, the grizzly will usually get as far away from you as possible. Surprised, a grizzly is apt to take offense. If the grizzly has cubs with her, she is more dangerous than dynamite and about as unpredictable as a tornado. Stay away from bears; they have killed more than a few humans in Glacier National Park.

Excursion boats are a fine way to enjoy the beauty of the park, and they are available at **Many Glacier, Rising Sun, Two Medicine** and **Lake McDonald.** Be sure to dress warmly even in mid-July because the breeze coming off those glacier-fed waters is apt to be mighty cool.

Guided horseback-riding tours are available at **Many Glacier, Lake McDonald Lodge** and at **Apgar** (west entry to park).

Four whitewater rafting companies offer all kinds of whitewater raft trips on the middle and north forks of the **Flathead River.** Incidentally, 219 miles of this wonderful river have been designated as "Wild and Scenic" by Congress.

Day hikers find a paradise here, with hikes of many different lengths and degrees of difficulty. Informational leaflets with maps of the trails are available at every **visitors' cen-**

ter, with the one at Apgar doing the most business. You can get a leaflet for $1 by writing to the Glacier Natural History Association, at West Glacier, MT 59936.

Dogs are absolutely prohibited on any hike in Glacier, for a very good reason. Grizzly bears will chase a dog and kill it if possible, and if a grizzly chases your dog, your dog will probably run yipping to you. The grizzly then may transfer his attention to you, with unfortunate results. Also, the dog is apt to get real brave when he gets close to his master. He might then turn to fight the grizzly and get killed. Dogs don't belong in Glacier Park and are prohibited if not on a leash.

Overnight camping and backcountry backpacking are allowed with a backcountry permit, available from the park rangers and at all visitors' centers. Because of the danger of meeting grizzly bears in the backcountry, this type of recreation is best reserved for the experienced hiker.

Wildlife viewing is one of the big attractions in this "place touched by magic." Special places to see mountain goats are at **Goat Lick** on Highway 2 and at the **Logan Pass Visitor Center** up on top. Another good spot for seeing goats is on the south side of **Mt. Grinnell** in the Many Glacier area.

Bighorn sheep are commonly seen on the mountainsides above the **Many Glacier Lodge** and campgrounds. Bighorns may be seen almost anywhere in the eastern half of the park, and if you use a good pair of binoculars, you can pick them out more easily. In the hottest part of summer, they like to find remaining snow patches and frequent windswept ridges for freedom from the insects that can make life miserable for them.

Less commonly seen, moose frequent low, marshy areas of the park. The best time to see them is in the very early morning. Both mule deer and whitetail deer are found in the park, along with the secretive, mostly nocturnal cougar, which is very seldom seen. The NPS in Glacier Park asks that you do nothing to interfere with the normal activities of the wild animal. For example, if an animal looks alarmed and moves away from you, you've come too close. The animals lived in Glacier Park long before we came along, and if we want them to thrive in this great wildlife preserve, we have to leave them alone as much as possible. Is it possible to do that and still "see" lots of wildlife? You bet your RV it is. Give the animals respect and a little distance, and you'll both get along just fine.

The one thing you must not miss is the Going to the Sun Highway. Drive it or ride in a rubberneck bus, but see it all.

A last word of warning: In mid-August 1992, I spent a wonderful week in Glacier. Temperatures were up in the 70s and even well into the 80s some days. The week after I left, Glacier Park got 6 inches of new snow. Plan for snowfall *any* day of the year.

For the answers to any and all of your questions, you can call **Glacier National Park offices** at (406) 888-7800. For information about summer bus tours, call **Glacier Park, Inc.** at **Glacier Park Lodge,** (406) 226-9311. For a more formal, interpretive tour of the park highlighting Blackfeet Indian culture and history call **Sun Tours** at 1-800-786-9220. For information about tours during October–April, call (602) 207-6000.

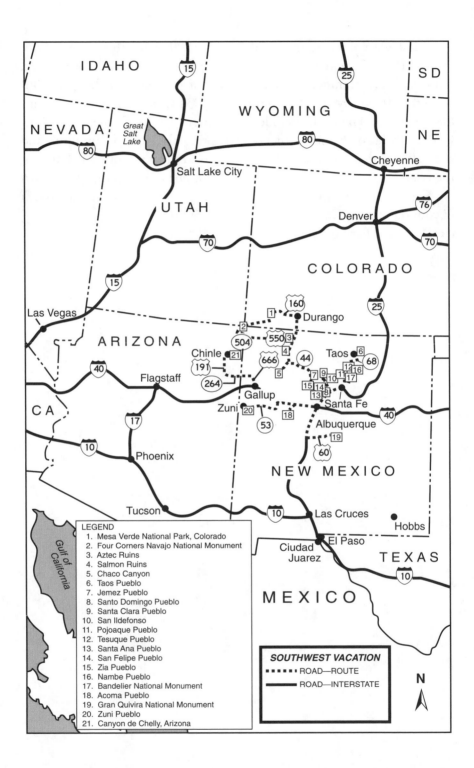

LEGEND

1. Mesa Verde National Park, Colorado
2. Four Corners Navajo National Monument
3. Aztec Ruins
4. Salmon Ruins
5. Chaco Canyon
6. Taos Pueblo
7. Jemez Pueblo
8. Santo Domingo Pueblo
9. Santa Clara Pueblo
10. San Ildefonso
11. Pojoaque Pueblo
12. Tesuque Pueblo
13. Santa Ana Pueblo
14. San Felipe Pueblo
15. Zia Pueblo
16. Nambe Pueblo
17. Bandelier National Monument
18. Acoma Pueblo
19. Gran Quivira National Monument
20. Zuni Pueblo
21. Canyon de Chelly, Arizona

SOUTHWEST VACATION

····· ROAD—ROUTE

—— ROAD—INTERSTATE

N

5
Indian Trails of Colorado, New Mexico and Arizona

Mesa Verde National Park

One of the most fascinating North American RV trips begins at Mesa Verde, Colorado, goes through western New Mexico and ends in Arizona. This trail may give you a few answers to the mysteries of our predecessors on this continent and leave many questions unanswered.

We start out on Highway 160 east of Cortez, Colorado. Watch for the intersection where the all-weather road turns off to the south, leading to the National Park Service headquarters for **Mesa Verde** ("green table"). We are going to visit the ruins

of the Anasazi civilization, which disappeared 200 years before Columbus started on his voyage of discovery.

Anasazi is a Navajo word meaning "the ancient ones." Once I asked a well-educated Navajo at what date his people came to the American Southwest. He replied, "About 1500 A.D." Then I asked him about the Anasazi and he said, "They were here in the beginning." Archaeologists believe that the Anasazi came to North America across the "Bering bridge," and so believe it's improbable that they were here "in the beginning." The Anasazi are, however, the earliest peoples we know about who lived in the Southwest.

The Anasazi came to Mesa Verde about A.D. 550—nomads who wanted to settle down. They chose this location because it offered sufficient water to grow crops and good enough soil to grow corn, which provided their best hope of surviving the "starving time" when heavy snows covered the area.

They built primitive pit houses, little more than roofed-over pits dug in the earth. As the centuries went by and their numbers increased, their buildings became much more permanent and much more beautiful, culminating in the precise stone masonry of the most interesting structures in the park—**Cliff Palace, Mug House, Long House** and the rest. Their most ambitious construction projects still survive for us to marvel at, with hand-cut masonry walls, precisely fitted corners and round kivas with ventilation shafts. Almost all of the buildings are situated under the protection of the red sandstone cliffs, with their courtyards facing into the winter sunlight for warmth.

They made excellent pottery vessels, primarily by coiling strands of wet clay around and around to form the vessel, then firing it for permanence. They were strongly religious, although we know little about the gods they worshipped.

It is obvious that they had a very good thing going here at Mesa Verde until the year A.D. 1275. That's when the rains stopped—for twenty-five years there was no appreciable precipitation, a drought that is chronicled in tree rings. Dendrochronology, the study of tree rings, provides compelling evidence that rain simply stopped falling from the heavens, which meant that crops withered and died under the summer sun, children went hungry, game became scarce, fruit and berry crops failed and people eventually abandoned their settlement. The evidence for this "drying out" theory to explain the disappearance of the Anasazi is incontrovertible at Mesa Verde, yet far to the south a similar exodus occurred at the same time, and the evidence is not as strong there. Maybe there was another reason for the disappearance of this culture that had flourished for more than a millennium. What do you think?

First stop must be the **Visitor Center** for orientation and to make sure you don't miss any of the attractions. If you come during peak visitation time, ask about the possibility of joining a trip out to **Wetherill Mesa**, thought to be an outlying settlement of the same culture. Bring lots of film and take your time as you explore the wonders of Mesa Verde. Try to get to know these sturdy people who eked out a living on this beautiful mesa for a thousand years—and if you figure out why they left, be sure to tell me, for I'm puzzled.

After exploring Mesa Verde, I'd suggest you drive over to **Durango,** a historic mining town where you can take a ride on the narrow-gauge railroad that once hauled treasure out of the mountains, and today provides a thrilling ride through high mountain scenery—it's called the Durango and Silverton and it's worth the time and trouble. Jeep rides into the high country near Durango are also available.

Four Corners National (Navajo) Monument

There is only one spot in the United States where the borders of four states come together at one point. The four states are New Mexico, Colorado, Utah and Arizona. Signposts point to **Four Corners National Monument.** But don't look for the U.S. National Park Service here. The National Monument is erected by the Navajo Nation. Here it's possible to put one leg in Arizona, your other leg in New Mexico, one hand in Colorado and one hand in Utah. Sound like a good place to have your picture taken? Thousands do, but please point your camera at the head end of that pose. Other-

Window Rock, the namesake of the town of Window Rock, headquarters of the Navajo Nation.

wise you could be accused of "mooning," and the picture won't show you at your photogenic best.

Navajo vendors offer their crafts from booths arranged around the monument. Navajo rugs and saddle blankets are beautiful, tightly woven and durable, and their value has gone up a hundredfold since they were first discovered by tourists about forty years ago. The Navajos are famed both for their woven products and for their turquoise and silver jewelry. The best places to shop for Navajo craftworks are probably in the shops at the **Zuni Pueblo,** or in stores in **Albuquerque** and **Farmington.**

Speaking of Farmington, this bustling town makes a good head-quarters for our next area of exploration. The "greater Farmington" area includes an excellent **KOA** at 1900 East Blanco in Bloomfield. I've enjoyed staying at **Mom and Pops Trailer Park** at 901 Illinois, right in Farmington. There's a good **River Grove Trailer Park** at 801 East Broadway, also right in town. Farmington offers everything you might want to purchase in its shopping malls. If you're going to visit Navajo Lake and State Park, you might be better served at **Riverside Park in Aztec** (the town) which is 15 miles northwest of Farmington on U.S. 550.

Navajo Lake State Park offers more than 200 camping spaces, 50 with water and electricity. The camping fee at the state parks is always $7 for developed campsites, and commercial campgrounds cost $9 and up.

Venturing forth from any one of these campgrounds, you'll want to visit the **Aztec Ruins,** which wins first prize in the "wrong name" championship. There never was any connection with the Aztec civilization in southern Mexico. The Aztec Ruins are only partially excavated, and some parts have been excavated and then backfilled to prevent the walls from falling down. The great

ceremonial kiva has been completely (and beautifully) reconstructed and is a "must see" for anyone interested in following the trail of the Anasazi, the ancient ones who first lived in the Four Corners area. The Aztec Ruins were located on the **Animas River** and were a place of refuge in the drought years. There is also evidence that commerce between Mesa Verde to the north and Chaco Canyon far to the south passed through Aztec. We don't know why it was abandoned, but local lore holds that it was never totally abandoned— Navajo bands used it intermittently after the original pueblo occupants had departed for reasons—and parts—unknown.

Next stop should be the **Salmon Ruins** on U.S. 64, 11 miles east of Farmington. The name belonged to a pioneer family who homesteaded the land. There's an excellent small museum that goes a step further in explaining some of the mysteries of the Anasazi culture. Unlike Mesa Verde and Chaco, the Salmon Ruins were only occupied for about sixty years, and even then they were abandoned at least three times. We really know very little about the movements of peoples in the period from A.D. 1200 to A.D. 1500. One of the fascinations about tracing the civilization of the Anasazi is that every new answer seems to raise at least two new questions.

When you first register at a campground in Farmington, or after you've completed your exploration of the Farmington area, take time to drive out to see **Shiprock**. This 1,700-foot-tall "rock with wings" is southwest of the town of Shiprock, about an hour's drive from Farmington. Perhaps you'll combine a trip there with a trip to the Four Corners National Monument.

Chaco Culture National Historic Park

Pueblo Bonito was once the largest city in North America. It was the center of a huge sprawling civilization with a far-flung system of surfaced roads (although the Anasazi did not use the wheel). To my mind, it represents the greatest riddle of the entire Anasazi story. Why was it placed in a barren area with very little rainfall and with poor soil? Even before the Anasazi set up shop there, they knew that the annual rainfall was insufficient to support a large population, yet they built cities there with a total population well above 15,000.

You reach **Chaco Canyon** by turning west off of Highway 44 at **Nageezi** and then driving 7 miles of blacktop and 17 miles of rough gravel road to reach the lovely blacktop roads inside the NPS domain. A second route leaves 44 on 57 at

Blanco. This road joins with the first a few miles farther west. Road maps show a third access from **Crown Point** far to the south. Please do not take this road! It is incredibly rough and not for RVs—it chews them up and spits them out.

Chaco Canyon has always been hard to get to, but the Chacoans got there in A.D. 300, and they flourished and prospered. They built increasingly larger and more complex buildings and constructed religious kivas, each more elaborate than its predecessor. They developed a trading empire that brought turquoise from **Cerillos** (near Santa Fe), shells from the Pacific Ocean and even imported food from the north when times were lean. They learned how to get the best crop production from their sandy soil, despite the scant rainfall, by using irrigation systems, small dams and terraces that caught

Looking down on the campground at Chaco Canyon.

the runoff from the infrequent rains and channeled it onto the alluvial fans where they grew crops. Although they utilized their scant rainfall to the utmost, it was never really sufficient for the growing population.

In their buildings, some as tall as five stories, they used layered rock construction and roofing beams made from 35-foot ponderosa pine logs. Those logs had to come from the nearest forest, which was 40 miles away. They must have been carried on the shoulders of men, for there were no pack animals and they didn't have the wheel.

The ancient Chacoans studied the stars and planets to guide them in aligning their buildings and in determining proper dates for planting crops. From their pictographs, we know that they charted the progress of Venus and Sirius, even the tiny Pleiades, as they moved

Pictographs like these can be found all over the land where the Anasazi once lived.

across the skies. Their "sun dagger" on **Fajada Butte** indicates that they kept track of the vernal and autumnal equinoxes. Chaco was the greatest civilization to flourish in what is now the United States, but it ended abruptly about A.D. 1300 for reasons we cannot explain.

There's an excellent **visitors' center,** operated by the U.S. National Park Service, and this should be your first stop, for orientation purposes. While you are this close, drive on past the visitors' center and claim a campsite at the small trailer park. No hookups, but we *are* self-contained, aren't we? I love this campground; where else can I sit in my comfortable coach and look out at pre-Columbian petroglyphs and homes that people lived in over seven hundred years ago?

Chaco Canyon is unusual in that the Park Service allows you to drive right up to the ruins you want to visit. Park your RV on the macadam parking lot and use the self-guided tour pamphlet to visit the most important parts of this huge place. Pueblo Bonito probably had six hundred rooms in its heyday! Where warning signs tell you to stay away, do what you're told. Some of the walls are in need of stabilization, but the money isn't available for restoration.

One of the most interesting satellites of Pueblo Bonito was named **Hungo Pavi.** We don't know the derivation of that name, but far to the west in Hopi Land there is a town called **Shongopavi**—there must certainly be a connection there.

A short drive along the good blacktop from the visitors' center and the **Una Vida Ruin** brings you to **Chetro Ketl**, second largest of all the Chaco ruins. This was definitely a "preplanned" community. They knew that the building would be of three stories before they started construction. It was not a case of "adding on," as seems to be the case in many other pueblo buildings in the Southwest.

The large house in Chetro Ketl was started in A.D. 1038 and finished in A.D. 1054. It had five stories and probably contained five hundred rooms, all sized for the small Anasazi. It is believed that the average adult male Anasazi was perhaps 5 feet tall. There's a huge ceremonial kiva, but you'll see an even bigger one at **Casa Rinconada.**

Leave your car in the Chetro Ketl parking lot and walk less than a quarter of a mile to **Pueblo Bonito,** largest of them all. Built on a precise semicircular design, sheltered by the towering sandstone bluff, most of its architectural splendor has survived the centuries. One section, however, was smashed flat when a huge chunk of the cliff fell on it. Completed about A.D. 1080, this is the supreme achievement of the Anasazi culture. In 1921 archaeolo-

gists financed by the National Geographic Society excavated here, clearing out six hundred rooms and thirty-three kivas.

Next stop is **Pueblo del Arroyo,** a great house built about the same time as Pueblo Bonito and Chetro Ketl. Here the archaeological excavation turned up brightly colored macaw feathers and evidence that the big parrots had been kept as pets. This surely suggests trade with what is now Mexico.

Turning back toward the visitors' center on the Ruins Loop Road, you come to the parking area where you leave your rig for the short walk to **Casa Rinconada,** and here you're allowed to enter the great kiva. Enter and sit quietly for a few minutes. Try to imagine what ceremonies took place in this great religious arena. Try to picture the Anasazi deciding the fate of the Chacoan civilization—a civilization that was contemporaneous with the Crusades in Europe and Asia, 200 years before the birth of Christopher Columbus. You must conclude that this was indeed a great civilization, one that began in pit houses as much as 5,000 years before the birth of Christ and became the largest city in ancient North America, and you'll wonder again why they disappeared.

Still curious? There's a 4-mile hiking trail, starting at **Casa Chiquita's** parking lot and leading to the **Penasco Blanco Ruin** (bring along drinking water). Near the campground, you'll find a bike trail that leads to the **Wijiji Ruin.** From **Kin Kletso,** you can climb to the top of the cliff and enjoy a long walk that allows you to look down on the ruins of Pueblo Bonito and Chetro Ketl. Here you'll see the remains of farming terraces that were the work of our earliest soil conservationists, the Chacoans.

You'll need at least two full days in Chaco Canyon to allow you to even begin studying it. But no matter how many days you invest in Chaco Canyon, you'll never solve the mystery and the magic of it—you'll have a million questions about this city in the desert, a city that was once the largest in North America.

If you're lucky enough to visit Chaco Canyon during a full moon, I urge you to walk out away from the campground noise, find a comfortable rock and just sit for half an hour. Let the ghosts of those former inhabitants speak to you, watch them as they work and play—all in your mind, of course. And if you're really lucky, the querulous and plaintive song of the coyote will drift in from the desert to enhance the magic of the moonlit night.

When Chaco Canyon's prosperous towns died, about A.D. 1300, these people didn't die. They moved to the south and to the west of Chaco or went east to find life-giving water along the Rio Grande. They didn't start new towns, but rather moved in with existing Pueblo peoples. Many of those pueblos are still occupied and thriving today. There is a concentration of living pueblos between **Albuquerque** and **Española.** I suggest you headquarter in or near Santa Fe and visit them.

Living Pueblos

Taos Pueblo, just 70 miles north of Santa Fe on good blacktopped highways, offers three separate attractions—all named Taos. First is the modern **city of Taos,** which is more than four hundred years old. It is a popular ski resort town, a famed artist's colony and the source of much of the history of the immediate area. This Taos was the home of Kit Carson, and there's a park named for him. It was also a terminus of the Santa Fe Trail. Second is **Ranchos de Taos,** a much younger suburb, which features the famous church that Georgia O'Keeffe loved to paint. Third is the much older suburb of **Taos Pueblo,** one of the oldest continuously occupied locations in North America. People have been living in the Taos Pueblo area since about 5000 B.C. The *Taosenos* have learned a lot from the white man—they now charge $5 to park your rig on the parking lot that butts up against the pueblo's big five-story communal dwelling, and they charge another $5 per camera if you want to take pictures. But it's definitely worth the money. This is a very photogenic spot—my favorite shot is taken looking across from the small creek toward the pueblo, with big white New Mexico clouds towering above.

There are several nice campgrounds in the Taos area, including the **Taos Valley RV Park,** 2 miles south of Taos, at about $24.50 for full hookups or $21.50 for water and electric hookups. They have 92 spaces—some of which are 60-foot pull throughs, (505) 758-4469. Also available are lots of U.S. Forest Service campsites—free! For information on U.S. Forest Service camping, telephone (505) 758-6200.

There are literally dozens of other living pueblos in the vicinity, small ones such as **Picuris** and **Pojoaque** and **Tesuque.** We can't visit them all, so we'll pick the ones that are most interesting.

Jemez Pueblo is reached by driving to San Ysidro on Highway 44, then turning north on State Highway 4. Although it is not as friendly toward tourists as Taos, it offers a good example of how the people have succeeded in maintaining their ethnic individuality and language, while surrounded by a sea of Anglos and Hispanics. While you're there,

An example of the pottery to be found for sale at the Taos Pueblo.

visit nearby **Jemez Springs,** the **Jemez State Monument Park,** the remains of a pioneer mission and the **Soda Dam** on Jemez Creek. Just to the north of the area you'll find pine-clad forests and lots of U.S. Forest Service camping facilities. We recommend the Indian bread, which is usually offered for sale by Native women along the side of Highway 4—different but delicious. Be sure to ask permission before you take any pictures—the Jemez people are sensitive about such matters. Respect their wishes; it is their home you're visiting.

Santo Domingo, one of the largest and most prosperous of the living pueblos, is just to the west of Interstate 25, halfway between Albuquerque and Santa Fe. The turn-off is well marked. The Santo Domingans farm an area of the Rio Grande flood plain, but almost all of them live on the communal pueblo itself. We suggest that you drive in, drive around the buildings on the outer streets—very slowly because of children playing—and then park by the church and go look at the paintings adorning its outer facade. Do not take pictures of the church; you might lose your camera if you do. Leaving the pueblo, drive to the famed trading post a mile away. Here you'll find authentic arts and crafts for sale, along with tawdry trinkets for the tourist trade. It's been my experience that you get what you pay for in this old trading post—at decent prices.

Santa Clara and **San Ildefonso** are both close to Española and not too far north of Santa Fe. Both are famed for their black-on-black pottery. Here lived "Maria, the Potter of San Ildefonso," who was memorialized in a book about her life and art. You'll find Native pottery for sale at many places. While near Santa Clara, you'll want to visit the **Puye Cliff Dwellings,** the earliest known homes of today's Santa Clarans. In both of these pueblos, remember to ask permission before you take photographs.

Along about here, you might want to visit **Pojoaque** (pronounced

Po-ho-ak-kee) and **Tesuque** (pronounced *Tuh-soo-kee*), both of which lie along Highway 285 north of Santa Fe and are receptive to tourist visits. The tiny pueblo of **Nambe** is also worth a visit. Have you seen "Nambe ware"?

Zia, Santa Ana and **San Felipe** are small pueblos easily reached by a short drive from either Santa Fe or Albuquerque.

Bandelier National Monument

Bandelier is reached by a short drive south and west of **Los Alamos,** the city where the atom bomb was developed and where much of Uncle Sam's nuclear research still takes place. A beautiful place, with the nation's greatest number of Ph.D.s per capita, Los Alamos is definitely not geared to the tourist trade but prefers to remain a rather secretive city.

The National Monument offers some glimpses into life of the earliest inhabitants. **Tyuonyi Ruins** are a short walk down a blacktopped trail from the visitors' center. Much of **Frijoles Canyon** is open to sightseers, and it is possible to visit the homes of the very earliest inhabitants, cut into the soft rock of the cliffs, and from that vantage point look down on the more impressive homes of the later period of their culture. My personal belief is that the people of Puye and of Tyuonyi came from Chaco Canyon when that area was abandoned about A.D. 1300.

If you're ambitious enough to take a moderately long walk, you can go see the carved stone mountain lions, believed to be the only statuary made by the Anasazi. There's an interesting museum and gift shop near the visitors' center, and some truly excellent artwork, is displayed there.

There's a good campground just inside the entrance to Bandelier National Monument that offers 98 spaces with drinking water and a dump station but no hookups. In the summer months it's usually filled up by noon, so sign up early.

After seeing Bandelier, drive back through Los Alamos and south through Santa Fe. There are several campgrounds available in that vicinity, or perhaps you might want to drive south of Santa Fe on Interstate 25 to reach **Albuquerque,** a city of half a million, which boasts several KOA campgrounds as well as other campgrounds.

From your Albuquerque headquarters, you'll want to visit **Isleta Pueblo** on the Rio Grande River just south of Albuquerque. It is easily reached by driving south on Interstate 25 and watching for the signs, or by leaving town on south Broadway and following the signs. The beautiful adobe church in Isleta is one of the oldest in North America.

The Isletenos are 95 percent Catholic but with a proviso. Years back, a Catholic priest named Stadtmueller had the courtyard of the church paved over. This aroused the ire of the Natives, who believed it was necessary to dance "in contact with the earth" when performing the ancient rituals, which they retained under their veneer of Catholicism. When the governor of the pueblo remonstrated Father Stadtmueller, he said, "It looks like you are trying to destroy the 'old way'." The priest retorted that he was trying to get rid of such pagan rites! Shocked and angered, the governor, himself a devout Catholic, arrested the priest and ousted him from the pueblo. In retaliation, the bishop of Santa Fe closed the church until "such time as the pueblo would apologize to Father Stadtmueller." Things remained at an impasse for several years, with the devout Isletenos walking to another church to attend mass on Sundays. Then the bishop was replaced by Archbishop Robert Sanchez, who was a native New Mexican and understood the Native beliefs. Bishop Sanchez quietly named a new pastor for Isleta and the church was reopened, bringing an end to the affair. Your visit to the ancient church will be welcomed as long as you behave with respect and don't disrupt services. It's well worth a look-see.

The **Indian Cultural Center,** just a block south of Interstate 40 on Twelfth Street N.W. in Albuquerque, offers wonderful exhibits telling the story of the nineteen Indian pueblos and plays host to over 300,000 visitors per year. Worth your visit.

While in Albuquerque, take a ride on the world's longest tramway at **Sandia Crest.** It provides a wonderful view of the city far below. For information call (505) 243-0605. There's plenty of parking at the lower terminal of the tram, even for big RVs.

Now I want to propose a side trip that will take a day or two, depending upon how interested you are in the ancient pueblos. Drive south of Albuquerque on Interstate 25 to the junction with State Road 60 at **San Antonio, New Mexico.** While you're in San Antonio, you might as well sample the "world's best hamburger" at the Owl Bar and Cafe, right on the corner. It's a green chili hamburger and it's great. Continue west on 60 to **Mountainair,** which is headquarters and visitors' center for **Salinas National Monument.** The National Monument administers the ruins of the former mission cities known as **Abo, Quarai** and **Gran Quivira.** These were once prosperous pueblos, but continual raids by the Comanches to the east led to their demise. They are towns that literally died of fear. Quarai is

the most beautiful, if you can only visit one. Gran Quivira is the largest and most impressive.

Next, we head west out of Albuquerque on Interstate 40 headed for **Acoma,** the Sky City. Continue 6 miles west of **Laguna** on Interstate 40. The turnoff is well marked, and the road to Acoma is blacktopped. This is one of the oldest continuously occupied locales in our country, having been home to Acoma Indians for about ten centuries. It is built atop a steep-walled mesa and was easily defended by the Acomas against other raiding tribes and the Spanish Conquistadores, but was finally breached by Hollywood, which talked them into allowing a road to be built to the summit so that heavy equipment could be brought up for the filming of a movie.

Go to the visitors' center and register for the next bus trip up the mesa. It'll cost you $7 per person and another $10 per camera, but it's well worth it. The beautiful **Catholic Church of San Esteban del Rey** is the top attraction here, although relations between the Acomas and the padres have not always been smooth. In fact, irate Acomans once threw their priest off the edge of the mesa to die on the rocks far below. A good visitors' center and small museum are also available.

There's a **KOA campground** 18 miles west of **Grants,** right on old

Route 66, boasting 50 pull throughs with all hookups. It costs $8.95 for two with all hookups. Phone is (505) 876-2662. Also recommended is the **Cibola Sands RV Park** on the Interstate 40 interchange going east out of Grants. It has 46 sites with full hookups and costs $17 per night for two people; (505) 287-4376.

This trip may be primarily about Indians, but that doesn't mean that you can't take time out to visit **El Malpais National Monument**— office right in Grants on main street—which is an old lava flow covering many square miles with solidified black remains of once molten rock. Several drives around the lava flows are available and give you a good look.

If you like, you can continue past the lava flows to the **Ice Caves** (they're on your highway map) or even go on past to **Zuni Pueblo,** one of the most interesting of all the living pueblos. Zuni is famed for its turquoise and silver jewelry, and you can watch the craftspeople as they produce their artistic pieces. If you want to buy Zuni crafts, or Navajo and Hopi crafts for that matter, Zuni is a good place to shop for truly authentic articles.

Whether or not you take the southern jaunt to Zuni, you'll return to Interstate 40 at **Gallup, New Mexico,** the "heart of the Indian country." Now we're going to leave

New Mexico and enter Arizona. The attractions ahead are too numerous to list—such as the **Hubbell Trading Post,** the **Petrified Forest, Meteor Crater**—they're all shown on your highway map, and you can visit as many as you like. But make *sure* that you see one place in this part of Arizona. Our grand tour of the Native lands *has* to include a visit to **Canyon de Chelly National Monument** on the big Navajo reservation.

To reach Canyon de Chelly (pronounced *Canyon du Shay*), turn north off Interstate 40 on Highway 191, stop briefly at **Hubbell Trading Post National Historic Site** and continue north to **Chinle** and the entrance to the Canyon de Chelly area. This area contains some of the most beautiful ruins left by the mysterious Anasazi—especially **White House Ruins.** Take your time here. To get the most beautiful pictures you'll probably have to take the whole day, so as to take advantage of the sun's movement to light your subject, which is built into niches on the steep walls of the red sandstone canyons. Be sure to stop at the visitors' center so that you'll know what you're seeing as you drive along the monument's roads. If you're in luck, you'll also see Navajos herding their sheep. Their purple velvet skirts and turquoise sunflower pendants just beg to be photographed, but be *doubly* sure that you ask permission before taking a Navajo's picture here. Some, especially the older ones, deeply resent having their picture taken.

There is much more to this story of the Anasazi and their successors, the many living pueblos of the Navajo and the Hopi. But you don't have that much time. You might want to continue north and west to see beautiful **Lake Powell,** formed by Glen Canyon Dam. Or you may be intrigued by place names like **Lukachukai, Tuba City, Keet Seel** or **Betatakin** or … the list goes on.

If you can hit only the high spots, by all means see Mesa Verde, Chaco Canyon, Bandelier, Taos and Canyon de Chelly. But I'll bet you'll be back to visit more of this intriguing and enchanting land of the mysterious Anasazi.

6
Utah's Magnificent Canyons

We started our tour of Utah's awesome red rock scenery with a visit to the buffalo herd!

The KOA 5 miles east of Monticello, Utah, was a welcome refuge after an autumnal hailstorm that left the ground temporarily covered with white but also provided relief from a very hot day. The skies cleared quickly, and we walked the quarter mile north to the buffalo pasture where we enjoyed watching the big shaggy beasts as they rolled in a dust bath, then strolled unconcernedly by, paying no attention to us on the other side of the fence.

Monticello was the starting point for a wonderful RV trip that was to take us to five national parks: Canyonlands, the Arches, Capital Reef, Bryce Canyon and Zion.

Canyonlands

First of all, be sure to visit the **Information Center** right in Monticello. It's just a long block south of the junction of Highways 191 and 666. A few miles north of Monticello on 191, turn to the left on Highway 211. The **Needles Visitor Center** should be your first stop, but the real destination is the road that leads to **Big Spring Canyon Overlook.** The magnificent scenery of the Canyonlands is the result of millennia of erosion, during which the

Colorado and Green Rivers carved the limestone layers into fanciful shapes, but the Big Spring Canyon overlook is as close as you're going to get to the confluence of these two rivers.

If you are young and determined, and an experienced desert hiker, you can travel to the **Confluence Overlook,** which gives you the chance to look down at the wedding of the waters far, far below.

There is plenty to look and marvel at from the **Wooden Shoe, Needles** and **Squaw Flat Overlooks.** There is primitive camping in this area, but be sure you check in with the rangers at the visitors' center before deciding to spend the night in the awesome silence and magnificent formations for which Canyonlands is justly famed.

After retracing your steps to Highway 191, go farther north and enter the road to the Needles Overlook. This scenic spot is outside of the Canyonlands Park, but affords a good viewpoint into the park itself.

There are many trailer parks in Moab, but early registration is recommended because of the twin attractions of Arches and Canyonlands. After making reservations, you are now ready to enter the northern section of the park. Drive north of Moab on 191, past the entrance to the Arches and turn back south on 313, which is marked as

the entrance both to Canyonlands and Dead Horse Point State Park.

Again visit the visitors' center to orient yourself with the drive south to **Grand View Overlook,** stopping at **Shafer Canyon Overlook, Bucks Canyon Overlook** and **Orange Cliffs Overlook.** Bucks Canyon is especially awesome, as it seems to rival the Grand Canyon in size and depth.

There's a campground and scenic overlook at the **Green River Overlook,** but the road into it is a very rough, jolting ride and there are so many wonderful vistas that we recommend you skip this one.

By now you've noticed that it is not possible to go in one end of Canyonlands and drive out the other. Geology dictates where a road is possible and where it is not possible to go with wheels. I asked the ranger if there would ever be a road connecting the southern and northern sections of the park, and his answer was, "I sure hope not." It is easy to agree that the rugged scenery can only be glimpsed and never experienced close up from your RV. There are 527 square miles of the Canyonlands National Park and most of it can be seen from paved roads. If you want close-up views, you'll need a stout four-wheel-drive vehicle or an experienced pair of hiking boots. Daytime high temperatures are something to keep in mind, and make sure that you have plenty of drinking water at all times, for the dry desert air seems to suck moisture out of your body.

Heading back north again, you should take the turnoff to **Dead Horse Point State Park.** There's a $5 entrance fee, but that's a bargain. One of the most spectacular views is that seen from the **Dead Horse Point Overlook.** Visit the visitors' center to learn how this point got its name. There is an excellent campground here in the state park. Half of the campsites can be reserved—as much as 120 days in advance—but the other half is first come, first serve. Sites covered by the reservation system are numbered 1-2-3-5 and 16 through 21. All reservations must be made at least three days in advance. For **Utah state parks information,** call 1-800-322-3770 toll free. You'll be talking to parks headquarters in Salt Lake City, which is connected by computer line to Dead Horse Point State Park. This campground fills up early, even after Labor Day. Our last visit found the campground full at 10:00 on a Monday morning in the latter half of September.

Whether you spend the night at Dead Horse Point Campground or at one of the commercial campgrounds in Moab, you should not be in a hurry to enter the Arches, because the east sun makes both travel and photography difficult in the first hour after sunrise. For more information about Canyonlands, write to Superintendent, Canyonlands National Park, 2282 South West Resource Boulevard, Moab, UT 84532-8000, or telephone (435) 259-7164.

The Arches National Park

A large salt bed underlies all of the land in the Arches National Park, but there is a deep layer of red rock on top of the salt. The weight of the red rock squeezed the salt in different ways, causing the red rock above it to split along "fin" lines. Some of the fins were forced upwards as much as 2,000 feet, other fins dropped into the salt layers. Erosion by wind, ice and water sculpted the fin-shaped red rock chunks into fanciful shapes, forming the greatest concentration of "arches" on the continent.

If my over-simplification of this fascinating geologic history leaves you with more questions than answers, stop at the **visitors' center** and study the exhibits there. Then go see for yourself. But before you go, unhook your trailer and leave it down here on the level. If you're towing a car behind your motor coach, leave the coach down here on the level. This is not to say that you cannot drive a large rig up the mountain— you definitely can. My ten-year-old

31-foot Southwind negotiated the climbs and turns without a problem. But the road is steep and narrow and the smaller rig fits into limited parking much better than the big rig.

Take the first three viewpoint turnouts and enjoy the view into the canyon of the Colorado far below. You'll be surprised at how much elevation you've earned in such a short drive. Next comes the **Petrified Dunes Viewpoint,** which affords a good look at the expanse of what appears to be sand dunes, but which is actually solid rock.

Just past the **Balanced Rock,** you take a right turn and head for the Windows section, where you can walk right up to both the **North** and **South Window Arches** and the **Turret Arch.** It's about one mile round-trip but doesn't seem that far over nearly level ground. If it's early morning, you'll be able to get good photographs of the Turret Arch, but the east sun will make it very difficult to photograph the two window arches. Maybe best to save those shots until the return trip when late afternoon sun makes these beautiful arches very photographable.

Next stop should be the **Wolfe Ranch,** where a pioneer actually eked out a living in this expanse of red rock for twenty years. Continue on to the **Delicate Arch Viewpoint** for a distant view of this beautiful formation. If you want to get closer,

return to the Wolfe Ranch and take the 3-mile walking trail to the foot of the arch itself. I call it an arduous walk, so be sure to take plenty of drinking water along—dehydration is a constant threat in this arid air. In the hottest part of the summer, afternoon temperatures may reach 110° Fahrenheit.

Back on the main road, you'll enjoy viewpoints at **Salt Valley Overlook** and **Fiery Furnace Overlook.** Continue on northward to **Devil's Garden,** which is the end of the "well-traveled" road. There's a campground here with 52 sites available on a first-come, first-serve basis, and it makes a fine base camp from which to visit—on foot—the most beautiful formation in the park, the delicate **Landscape Arch.** It's 0.8 of a mile each way, and on the same trip, you can visit **Tunnel** and **Pine Tree Arches.** For the young and physically fit, there is a continuing trail past Landscape to **Dark Angel** and **Double "O" Arches.**

Now you've seen the best of the Arches Park, so it's time to reverse directions and head back south. Afternoon sun now provides much better lighting for photographs in the Windows section.

The Arches has an entrance fee, and when you pay your fee, or display your Golden Age Passport, you'll be given a map of the park. This park map shows the roads we've described in red, and they'll give you no trouble. The same map also shows roads in black, like the Salt Valley Road, which leaves the main (red) road near Sand Dune Arch. Don't try these black roads in any RV. My recommendation is for four-wheel-drive vehicles only. If you want to see these remote parts of the park, talk to the park information desk about jeep trips with experienced guides and outfitters. And above all, take along plenty of water, for this country sure dries up every drop in your body.

A word of warning about pets. They must be under physical restraint at all times, and are *not allowed* on any trails. It is cruel to leave pets in a car where the noonday sun may raise the temperature to killing heat.

There are several excellent commercial campgrounds in Moab, but they are operating at full capacity during the months from May through September. It is wise to get your campsite early, then do your sightseeing secure in the knowledge that you have a place to stay when your long day is finished.

You'll run out of time before you run out of arches, for there are more than 2,000 of these spectacular formations in the park. Although I've visited the Arches several times, I feel that I've seen less than half of the beauty it offers, which is just another reason for coming back.

For more information about the Arches National Park, write to the Superintendent, Arches National Park, P.O. Box 907, Moab, UT 84532, or telephone (435) 259-8161.

Capitol Reef National Park

Leaving the Arches, you drive north on 191 about 30 miles to the junction with Interstate 70, then 20 miles west on the Interstate to the town of **Green River** where you'll find good campground facilities, restaurants, gas stations and almost anything else the RV traveler might need. Stock up if you need anything because we're heading for the boondocks. Eight miles west of Green River turn south on State Road 24. Next comes 44 miles of road that is definitely not a scenic byway. Although the road is in good condition, you'll meet few other rigs on this road where the monotony is best relieved by the sight of a coyote skulking across the road ahead of you.

That 44-mile stretch ends at Hanksville, where the Fremont River paints a wide green ribbon across the desert. Highway 24 is much more pleasant the rest of the way into Capitol Reef National Park, and changes dramatically once inside the national park. The Fremont River becomes a sparkling, mountain-fed stream, even featuring a sizable waterfall a short distance into the park.

The entrance to Capitol Reef National Park.

It's hard to explain the formation of Capitol Reef. Basically, tremendous geologic pressures forced a giant wrinkle to form across Utah. This giant wrinkle, stretching more than 100 miles, is properly called an "anticline" but this one wears the popular name of "waterpocket reef." As unbelievable forces shoved sedimentary layers up into this gigantic fold, many layers were stood on end, or tilted on their sides. Wind and water erosion over the millennia sliced off top sections of the reef, forming strange rock formations, some beautiful, like the formation that gives the park its name, some grotesque or even comical. The Fremont River cuts a snaky path across the reef, and that allowed for construction of Highway 24 across the park.

The first point of interest is the **Behunin Cabin,** built by an early Mormon settler who farmed the tillable sides of the river until repeated flooding destroyed his fields, forcing him to abandon the farm. Tiny as the cottage was, it was home to no fewer than ten family members. It is told that the boys slept in an undercut section of the canyon wall, and the young girls slept in the wagon box.

Next comes the **Capitol Dome,** a white formation which bears a resemblance to the dome of the U.S. Capitol building, and some interesting petroglyphs high on the canyon wall—seemingly safe from vandalism. It would be hard to get a good photograph of the petroglyphs because you can't possibly get close.

Also in this area the park preserves the historic **Fruita schoolhouse.** The town got its name from the fruit orchards sustained by irrigation from the life-giving Fremont River, orchards that still produce fruit today.

Highway 24 takes us directly to the **visitors' center.** After visiting these exhibits, take the scenic drive southward to take a good look at the **Fruita Campground,** 71 sites available to RVs as well as tents, on a first-come basis. Twelve miles of scenic drive brings you to the **Egyptian Temple** and the **Golden Throne** formations and a short hike allows access to **Capitol Gorge.**

For more information about Capitol Reef National Park, write to the Superintendent, Capitol Reef

National Park, Torrey, UT 84775.

Because the Fruita Campground was full during our last visit, we discovered a real gem of a trailer park on the western edge of the small town of **Torrey**, just 5 miles out the western entrance to the park. Called **Thousand Lakes Campground**, it is a big, spacious, well-laid-out park, with full hookups, a big swimming pool, steak dinners if ordered in advance and lots of green grass, which is especially welcome in this semi-desert environment. We arrived an hour before sundown and promptly turned on the air conditioner. At sundown we turned it off and opened everything up to a fine breeze as we broke out the lawn chairs to enjoy the serenade that accompanied first dark. Coyotes sang their ventriloquial song from the north, while farm dogs answered from the west. Before morning, all windows were closed and the furnace cut in, which is typical weather in the bone-dry desert country. When the sun goes down, the temperature plummets swiftly.

After touring three national parks in the canyon country, you may think you've seen it all. Not so; hang onto your hats for the best is yet to come.

Bryce Canyon National Park

Leaving Torrey, Utah, on Highway 12, you soon enter the **Dixie Na-tional Forest**, a land of steep climbs, pine-clad mountains, sweeping vistas and wildlife. The road climbs and curves all the way up to a summit of 9,200 feet above sea level, about 4,000 feet higher than the town of Torrey. We can count on seeing several mule deer each trip, especially in the early morning hours. This stretch of road is known as the **Clem Church Memorial Highway** and is designated as a scenic byway. All of the viewpoint turnoffs are worthy of a short stop, for the scenery is magnificent.

After leaving the Dixie National Forest, you pass through the tiny settlement of Boulder, and now the road gets truly interesting. It follows the very thin top of a ridge, with steep drop-offs to either side. At times the ridge is so narrow that there is barely room for the highway. Don't misunderstand—the road is perfectly safe and in good condition, but the driver will not be gawking around, he or she will have eyes only for the road.

Stay with Highway 12 to Highway 63, which will take you to the entrance of Bryce Canyon, the most colorful of all national parks. This is a fee area, of course, so have your Golden Age Passport ready. A word of warning is in order here—check your supply of color film and replenish it at the **visitors' center** for you are about to enter the most vividly colored national park. Now, if you can leave your trailer outside, please do so. Although road improvement projects completed in late September 1995 have brought the roads more in line with today's needs, Bryce Canyon is nearing three million visitors annually, and there can never be enough parking. Also, trailers were not permitted past Sunset Point on our last visit there. NPS campgrounds are available at both **North** and **Sunset Campgrounds** on a first-come basis.

There are two different turnoffs to **Sunrise** and **Sunset Points** and a walking trail connecting the two. If you plan an "in-depth" look at Bryce Canyon, by all means take the hike between the two. But the next at-

The entrance at Bryce Canyon National Park.

traction, **Inspiration Point,** is the most beautiful place in the park in my humble opinion. All three viewpoints give you a good look into the multicolored giant formations carved by wind and water and frost, which are the most interesting parts of Bryce Canyon itself.

Next comes **Bryce Canyon Point** itself, where the **Under the Rim hiking trail** has its beginning. This 22 miles of hiking trail is not for the out-of-condition person, as it has changes in elevation of as much as 3,000 feet. Again, this is dry country and hikers must carry along sufficient drinking water for their own needs. Hikers attempting any of the backcountry trails need a free permit available from the ranger stations or the visitors' center.

Some parts of Bryce Canyon can be viewed from horseback trails. If you're a horseman, write to Bryce-Zion Trail Rides, P.O. Box 128, Tropic, UT 84776, or telephone (435) 679-8665. A much easier way of getting from Bryce Canyon Point to **Rainbow Point** is available via the newly improved road leading south to **Swamp Canyon,** which affords a beautiful view of the tremendous gullies and formations below. This is also the starting point for a walking trail that connects to the Under the Rim Trail.

Then it's on to **Natural Bridge,** an arch formation formed by freezing and cracking, rather than by erosion by wind and water as most natural arches are; to **Agua Canyon** with its immense panorama of vertical cliffs; and **Ponderosa Canyon** with the "hoodoos," which are one of the trademarks of Bryce Canyon National Park. Hoodoos are vertical free-standing pillars of varicolored rock that invite the eye to imagine ghosts, or hobgoblins or anything else the fertile imagination can dream up.

You're nearing the end of this long, lovely trail. Rainbow Point marks the turnaround spot for vehicles. Here you'll want to photograph the "poodle" formation, which looks like a posing poodle. But perhaps you are already out of color film, for surely the sheer walls, fantastic formations, far vistas and pine forests are too tempting for the photographer to pass up.

From Rainbow Point there is nowhere to go except back the way you came. But you'll find a very different lighting scheme on the northbound trip, for the sun has changed its angle and the more westerly lighting opens up entirely new vistas across the majestic canyons. What was formerly in shadow is now in bright sunlight and vice versa. This is especially true of the views from Bryce Canyon Overlook. Where did the name come from? Ebenezer Bryce, a Mormon pioneer, came to

Paria Valley in 1875 and prospered for a time by harvesting pine trees from the plateau. His neighbors called the canyon behind his home Bryce's Canyon and from this came the name of the national park.

For more information about Bryce Canyon, write to the Superintendent, Bryce Canyon National Park, Bryce Canyon, UT, 84717 or telephone (435) 834-5322.

Zion National Park

Before we try to help you visit Zion National Park, let me state that you should not enter the park in a motor coach of more than a 21-foot length, nor should you pull a trailer into the park. The reason is the tunnel. No, not the short and easy first tunnel on the way in—we mean the 1.1-mile-long second tunnel. Because the tunnel is circular in cross section, the motor coach cannot travel down the right lane, but must drive down the middle of the road. This means that the motor coach must be given preference over all other travel, which means stopping traffic and holding it while your motor coach comes through. To stop traffic means inconveniencing all other traffic. Bending over backwards to allow entry to the park, the National Park Service *will* stop traffic and let you ride right down the center of the tunnel, straddling both lanes. To do this service, the NPS charges you $10. This is explained to the RV driver on a billboard on the way into the park, and again by the ranger at the entrance station where you pay your entrance fee (or show your Golden Age Passport). After you pay your $10, they hang a big yellow ribbon permit inside your windshield. When you approach the tunnel, the traffic control person will signal you to the side. Using radio to communicate with the traffic controller at the other end of the tunnel, you are waved on—right down the middle of the long tunnel.

It's not as complicated as it seems, and I took our 31-foot Southwind through last September. However, if you can travel by any other means, you should do so. Parking is limited at the Visitor Center and at Zion Lodge, and your big RV takes up a lot of room. Mine sure did.

Most of the beautiful scenery of the four parks already mentioned is seen from the top, looking down into the colorful depths of mighty canyons. Zion is definitely different. Instead of looking down, you *go* down … more than 1,200 feet down via five sharp switchback turns of the asphalt road down to the valley floor where you'll visit the **visitors' center** to orient yourself.

Then drive north on the park road to **Zion Lodge**, where you'll park your rig and ride the tram cars to see the most spectacular part of this national park. Tickets for the tram cars cost $2.95 per person and are on sale at Zion Lodge. Let the veteran driver handle the wheel as you relax to enjoy the awesome cliffs, shaded river vistas and unbelievable steep walls. In Zion, you'll definitely be looking up rather than down. You'll see hikers and climbers far up on the steep sides of the canyon walls, and you'll be amazed at the stupendous formations, especially those that got their fanciful names from an early Methodist minister — the **Great White Throne, Angels Landing** and so forth. The tram cars stop at the most gigantic formation, the **Temple of Sinawava**, a vast semicircular amphitheater of red rock. The stop at the Temple is long enough to allow you to take a few photographs, but if you wish to stay longer, just tell the driver, and he'll give you a ticket to reboard another tram one hour later.

The end of this road is the beginning of the **Narrows hike**, 16 miles round-trip, which follows (and wades through) the **Virgin River.** The Park Service classifies this hike as "strenuous," and they mean it. It is hard to believe that this tiny stream actually carved Zion Canyon, but it did. After the infrequent heavy rains, the Virgin becomes a raging torrent, and the hiking trail becomes impassable and very dangerous.

Campgrounds are available on a first-come basis at **Watchman** and at **South Campground,** both located south of the Main Visitor Center near the south entrance into the park (from Springdale). The Watchman is an imposing formation that rears its rocky head 6,545 feet above sea level.

Although most visitors see only the Zion Canyon sector, which we've just described, there is another spectacular portion of the park called the **Kolob Canyon** area. This farthest northwestern area of the park is accessible from Highway 15. There's another smaller **visitors' center** here, which specializes in information about the finger canyons of the Kolob. The Kolob Canyon Road leads to the **Kolob Canyon Overlook,** which is a splendid viewpoint.

But Zion National Park will not allow access to its greatest attractions to anyone but the hiker. The RV and auto travelers will see enough to keep them happy, and even if you have to stick to car trails, you will feel amply rewarded. But the hiker can enter another world of splendid isolation, inspiring beauty and majestic formations.

Hiking trails are grouped into ten different areas, and range from "easy" to "strenuous" with lengths of a half a mile round-trip to 28 miles round-trip. Backcountry hikers are required to get a free permit so that their destination is known to park authorities. Remember that this is the hot, arid Southwest and drinking water must be carried on all hikes.

By the way, if you want to exit from Zion Canyon the way you came in, you still have your permit to make the return trip without paying again.

For more information about Zion National Park, write to the Superintendent, Zion National Park, Springdale, UT 84767-1099, or call (435) 772-3256.

This trip has taken you through five great national parks, all within the red-rock country of Utah, but the five have many differences. Canyonlands surpasses them all in providing endless vistas; its sheer distances are almost beyond belief. The Arches has more beautiful natural bridges than any place on earth. Capitol Reef is an unique geologic showcase unlike any other. Bryce Canyon excels in colors of its grotesquely beautiful formations, its shadowed canyons and pastel-hued cliffs, while Zion offers the opportunity to look up at rainbow-colored cliffs from the comfort of shaded river banks. My personal favorite is Bryce Canyon, but that's only one man's opinion. Take a trip through these five, and you'll see a wonderful part of America the Beautiful.

7
A Taste of Texas

Texas is huge, distances are formidable, but the road system is one of the nation's best; campgrounds are available everywhere and there is so much to see. In this chapter, we want to give you a taste of Texas. Let's start in **San Antonio,** one of the most historic, most cosmopolitan, most interesting cities in the United States of America.

We usually headquarter at **Travelers World,** a good trailer park at 2600 Roosevelt Avenue. Maybe that's just out of force of habit; for many years we formed caravans there, heading for Mexico. But it is a very good trailer park, well laid out and with all amenities. Perhaps its biggest asset is the fact that it is on the bus line. You can take bus 42 right in front of the park entrance and get to downtown attractions quickly. Bus costs 75¢ per trip. Travelers World telephone is 1-800-755-8310. Locally, dial 532-8310. Reservations are definitely recommended.

Another excellent park is the **San Antonio RV Park,** also called **Admiralty Park,** which is right next to **Sea World,** on the west side of the city. There's a free shuttle to Sea World and express bus service to downtown. There are 240 paved sites, with all amenities. Be sure to call ahead for reservations, toll-free number is 1-800-999-7872.

Alamo KOA offers 350 shaded sites with the usual KOA amenities. Telephone is 1-800-833-5267. Located at 602 Gembler, it is just a few blocks off of Interstate 35. There are many others, so you should have little trouble in finding a trailer park.

There is so much to see that it is difficult to decide where to start. The most famous attraction is the **Alamo,** right in the heart of the city. Here Mexican forces took the fort after the Texans fought to the last man in an unparalleled example of heroism. You can walk through the Alamo buildings, see the historic exhibits, enjoy just sitting on a bench under the shade of the ancient live oak trees, read the story of the heroic battle that took place here. But don't make jokes like, "There never would have been a Texas if there had been a back door to the Alamo." Texans take their history seriously, and the Alamo is a real shrine to a group of real heroes. Treat it with respect.

After visiting the Alamo, you might want to have lunch at the historic **Schilo's Delicatessen**. It is a very popular place, always crowded and noisy, but the service is quick and the food is good, specializing in German fare.

Schilo's is right on the famed **Riverwalk,** and you will enjoy walking along its shady banks, or better yet, take a ride on a riverboat with a narrator to point out the sights. They'll even serve you lunch aboard the riverboats.

Remember that the Alamo was a working Catholic mission, and you'll want to see the other missions— **Concepcion, San Jose, San Juan** and **Espada.** Currently San Antonio is working on a 10-mile-long Mission Trail that will lead to all of these historic missions, which lie near the San Antonio River. All of these missions are worth a visit, but we especially recommend Mission San Jose, which is just a half mile or so from Travelers World trailer park.

A good way to see the sights is with a **Texas trolley ride,** a 75-minute tour that takes you to the Alamo, Rivercenter Mall, Hemisfair Park, King William Street, San Fernando Cathedral, the Riverwalk, El Mercado Farmers' Market, historic La Villita, the Institute of Texan Culture and the Palace of the Spanish Governors, which dates back to 1722. Cost is $7.50 for adults and $4.50 for children under 12. You board the trolley tour at the Alamo Visitor Center, right in the center of town. Ask about a "hop" pass, which allows you to leave the trolley at any one of its designated stops, spend as much time as you like and then reboard without added cost.

Although San Antonio history is mostly Hispanic, the German people who came to the Alamo city

Located downtown along a 2.5-mile section of the San Antonio River, the River Walk, or Paseo del Rio, hugs the banks of the river 20 feet below street level, offering visitors and local residents a picturesque collection of shops, hotels and night clubs. Photo by San Antonio Convention & Visitors Bureau.

in the mid-1800s left their mark. German merchants who prospered in flour milling and other industries built their lovely big homes on **King William Street,** which became one of San Antonio's most desirable areas. The trolley tour takes you by these big houses with their elaborate gardens. Today only one of these historic homes is open for public visit, the **Steves House.**

Sea World is one of the greatest attractions in San Antonio. Featuring killer whales, beluga whales, more than two hundred penguins, performing porpoises, a water park complete with slides and other children's delights, even the famous Budweiser Clydesdales are on display. For up-to-the-minute information and admission prices, telephone (210) 523-3611.

San Antonio's zoo ranks among the nation's best. Located in **Brackenridge Park** (with its floral gardens), there is a miniature railroad to carry you to various destinations. Well-arranged walking tours take you to see the animals and birds and reptiles. The zoo is open seven days a week, all year long.

If you want to see the entire city at a glance, go to the top of the **Tower of the Americas,** built for Hemisfair. We don't need to tell you where it is because it is visible from almost every part of the city. Believe it or not, there's a restaurant revolving around the top of the tower so you can admire the beautiful city while enjoying a meal.

Got time for a round of golf? There are five municipal courses. **Brackenridge Park** is a par 72, 6,185-yard course, (210) 226-5612; **Mission del Lago,** par 72, 7,150 yards, (210) 627-2522; **Olmos Basin,** par 72, 7,208 yards, (210) 826-4041; **Riverside,** par 72, 6,894 yards, (210) 533-8371; and **Willow Springs,** par 72, 6,602 yards (the second hole is a par 5 of 663 yards), (210) 226-6721.

There are dozens of good "country club" type courses in and around the city; call the **San Antonio Convention and Visitors' Bureau** at 1-800-447-3372 and ask for the **San Antonio Golfing Guide** for full information about golfing opportunities in the area.

There's so much more to see and do in and around San Antonio, but you'll enjoy discovering it by yourself. The **Alamo Visitor Center** just to the west of **Alamo Plaza** can give you maps and informational leaflets about many more locations, and they are very knowledgeable about how to get to the city's attractions. We haven't even mentioned the Witte Museum, the San Antonio Museum of Art, the Botanical Gardens, the McNay Art Museum, the Yturri-Edmunds House and Mill, the Lone Star Brewery's Buckhorn Museum with its amazing display of horns and antlers, horse racing at Retama Park, and so much more.

You'll never see everything in San Antonio, but when it comes time to tear yourself away, take Interstate 37 south to Corpus Christi.

Corpus Christi calls itself the "Isle of Texas," which is a good indication of its many seaside attractions. We usually find ourselves at **Padre Island Trailer Park** and drive back and forth to this fascinating city. Last time we stayed at **Padre Palms Travel Park**, which offers eighty spaces. We liked being so close to the long fishing pier, which juts out into the water. All daylight hours the planes from the Naval Air Station roar overhead, but who cares —we're out sightseeing anyway. The place gets really quiet after dark. Telephone is 1-800-552-6250. Other trailer parks in the immediate vicinity are **Puerto del Sol Trailer Park,** (512) 882-5373, and **Colonia del Rey,** (512) 937-2435.

Padre Palms Travel Park is just a mile across the high bridge from two inexpensive seafood restaurants— **Snoopy's** and **Frenchies.** To reach them, turn to the right immediately after crossing the high bridge. At Snoopy's we ordered from the menu on the wall and then ate on the dock, watching the traffic on the Intracoastal Waterway.

A good way to start our exploration of Corpus Christi is a **sight-seeing cruise** on the bay. Drive to the Corpus Christi waterfront, at the T-head docks on Peoples Street, and board the 400-passenger paddle wheel steamer for a tour of the waterfront. The fall and winter schedule calls for 3:00 P.M. sailings on weekdays and many trips on Saturdays and Sundays. Tickets are $7 for adults and $4 for children. Be sure to call ahead and confirm times and costs. Telephone is (512) 884-1693 or (512) 884-8306.

Captain Clark's Flagship is a great way to tour the sights along the beautiful downtown bayfront.

If you prefer art to boats, visit the **Art Center** right on the Shoreline Drive. There's no charge for admission and much to see, including the opportunity to watch artists at work on their paintings. The center is open Tuesday through Sunday. Telephone is (512) 884-6406.

Back to the water, we recommend the **Dolphin Connection,** which will take you out to watch wild dolphins at play, at a cost of $17 per adult, $12 for children. Trips daily, weather permitting. For more information, call (512) 882-4126.

The **Water Street Market,** a fascinating array of shops and restaurants, is located just a couple of blocks away from Shoreline Drive, north of the T-head docks. Whether you are shopping for gifts and souvenirs, or wish to enjoy a good seafood meal, this is a good place to spend a few hours.

The **Museum of Science and History,** located near the Ship Channel, features exhibits of Padre Island Spanish shipwrecks and special exhibits for children. This is a "hands-on" place, and the youngsters love it. While in the area visit the ships of **Columbus's fleet,** the *Niña, Pinta* and the *Santa Maria.* Built by the Spanish government to commemorate the 1492 voyage to the Americas, these full-size replicas were docked in Corpus Christi for their final resting place. You can go on board, even go below decks to inspect these historic vessels. They are right under the bridge over the ship channel.

Across the Ship Channel Bridge, you'll find the **Texas State Aquarium,** featuring an albino alligator (the only one in the world on display), endangered sea turtles, shark exhibits and loads of fun for adult and child alike. There is an admission fee of $8 for adults. Telephone is 1-800-477-GULF. Open year-round.

Just a short hop from the aquarium, you can visit the **USS** *Lexington,* famed aircraft carrier of World War II. Admission is $7 for senior and military citizens, adults are $9 and children are $4. The *Lexington* is the most famous ship of the late, unlamented, world war. It was in most of the important battles in the war against Japan and survived numerous torpedoes. This is a hands-on chance to learn about history. For more information, telephone (512) 888-4873.

Need a little exercise? Corpus Christi offers several fine municipal golf courses. **Oso Beach Golf Course** is at 5601 S. Alameda, (512) 991-5351. **Gabe Lozano Sr. Golf Center** is at 4401 Old Brownsville Road, (512) 883-3696. There are also several good "country club" type courses, and you can get a list of these from the Chamber of Commerce in Corpus Christi.

As you would expect from its oceanfront location, Corpus Christi is a mecca for saltwater anglers. For starters, why not try your hand at a party-boat trip aboard the *Adventurer*. This boat is large and stable, an 85-foot twin diesel craft. No license is required, and the ship will even furnish tackle if you left yours at home. An eight-hour trip costs you $60, a 12-hour trip is $75. If you fail to catch a legal fish, you'll receive a voucher good for half price on another sailing. The delicious red snapper is the main target for these offshore fishermen. For more information, call (512) 854-1135.

In addition to the "head boats," there are many sportfishermen available in the Corpus Christi area: telephone Captain Clark at (512) 884-4369, Captain Don Hand at (512) 993-2024, or any one of a dozen

more. The Chamber of Commerce can furnish a complete list of sportfishermen, guides and pier- and jetty-fishing opportunities.

When you've finished seeing the sights in Corpus Christi, you have to cross over the bridge, the same high bridge you took to eat seafood at Snoopy's. Take a turn to the left when routes divide—it is clearly marked—and head for **Port Aransas.** The other direction leads to **Padre Island National Seashore,** which is 110 miles of a narrow strip of sand separating the Gulf of Mexico from the Laguna Madre. The best of Padre Island can be reached only by four-wheel-drive vehicle, so most of us senior citizens turn toward Port Aransas.

You are now on **Mustang Island.** Take the time to investigate **Mustang Island State Park** by taking one or two of the access roads leading to the beaches on the Gulf

The Texas State Aquarium.

side. This seemingly empty waste-land is teeming with bird species associated with beach habitats. For more information about Mustang Island State Park, write to P.O. Box 326, Port Aransas, TX 78373, or telephone (512) 749-5246.

Port Aransas is a very interesting place, a mecca for anglers of all types, a bird-watchers' haven, a source of good seafood and lots of opportunity for simply relaxing and enjoying the winter sunshine. But make sure of your reservations at a trailer park, because they are almost always filled to overflowing.

We stayed at the **Island RV Resort,** telephone is (512) 749-5600. They offer 109 spaces and all the amenities, but they are usually filled with fishermen and their families. **On the Beach RV Park** has 60 spaces. Their phone is (512) 749-4909, or 1-800-932-6337. And don't forget that Mustang Island State Park is only 14 miles away from Port Aransas. They offer 48 spaces.

Once you've solved the overnight camping problem, Port Aransas is headquarters for all kinds of fishing from deep-sea charters to party boats to pier and jetty fishing. On our last trip aboard a party boat out of **Deep Sea Headquarters,** red snapper limits were plentiful and included three fish over twenty-five pounds ... now that is some fine eating and great sport. Advance res-

ervations are almost always required and the **Deep Sea** folks can be reached at 1-800-705-3474 or (512) 749-5597. **Dolphin's Docks, Inc.,** also has a toll-free number, 1-800-393-3474. They offer fishing trips starting as low as $35. While driving around, you'll notice lots of fishermen fishing without a boat, from jetties and piers, and that kind of fishing is free. One of the nicest things about vacationing in Port Aransas is the bus route 94, also known as the Port Aransas shuttle. It can be boarded anywhere along the route, it's free and it takes you to every corner of the town—they've even got room for your lawn chair and fish cooler if you're heading for some jetty fishing.

Bird-watchers find Port Aransas and vicinity a real paradise. Depending upon the time of the year, you'll seek out the caracara, reddish egret, white-tailed hawk, buff-bellied hummingbirds—even the magnificent frigate bird. You'll see advertisements for boat trips to see the world's rarest bird, the whooping crane, but we advise you to wait until you get to the Rockport-Fulton area, where you'll spend less time going to and from and more time on the whooping crane area.

Not the least of Port Aransas attractions is the endless beach on the Gulf of Mexico side. Here's a chance to get off by yourself and enjoy the winter sun, the clean salt air and the abundant bird life. I can spend hours at the docks just looking at boats moored there, and hours watching the ship traffic on the Intracoastal Canal. When filled with Port Aransas, you'll leave the island town via a free ferry across to Aransas Pass. It's a very short trip on placid waters and it operates twenty-four hours a day. Our next stop is at Fulton, on the north end of Rockport. Take Highway 35 to get there.

One of the most pleasant campgrounds we enjoyed on our trips to the Texas Gulf Coast was located in **Fulton,** which joins Rockport on the north side. The **Sand Dollar Motel and RV Park** is a large, well-laid-out park with about 100 spaces, half of which offer cable TV. We always ask for site 83 where we can pull in under the deep shade of an ancient live oak tree. Be warned, however, that when you come in November, the slightest breeze will bring down a hail of acorns on your rig's roof. On our last visit we paid only $16 per day, which included cable TV. Their telephone is (512) 729-2381. There are several other trailer parks in the area so you should have no problem in that regard. Here are a few other selections: **Bahia Vista RV Park,** (512) 729-1226; **Beacon RV Park,** (512) 729-3906; **Driftwood RV Haven,** (512) 729-2452; and **Watersedge RV Park,** (512) 729-1100.

Directly across the street from the trailer park is the **Sand Dollar Pavilion,** which offers a good seafood menu. Also at the Sand Dollar Pavilion is the office and dock for the *Skimmer,* the boat that takes bird-watchers on a three-hour trip to see the world's rarest birds, the endangered whooping cranes. Captain Ted Appell has the eyes of a hawk, the ability to spot and recognize birds at a distance and the local know-how to get you within camera range of the rare cranes. He can even spot and explain the difference between the elegant tern, the caspian tern and the common tern. On November 13, we observed no fewer than eighteen whooping cranes and identified fifty-seven bird species in all. The *Skimmer* trip is a very pleasant experience because the specially designed craft can operate in 15 inches of water, is glassed in against the weather, offers comfortable inside seating, serves complimentary hot and cold beverages and even breakfast rolls, provides binoculars for those who want them and includes the very knowledgeable comments of Captain Ted.

There are two trips a day while the whooping cranes are in residence on their wintering grounds, at 7:45 A.M. and again at 1:30 in the afternoon. The trip costs $28 per person and is a real bargain. No tours on Tuesday, and reservations are a very good idea at all times. Telephone is 1-800-338-4551.

If you take the whooping crane boat trip in the morning, you'll have time in the afternoon to visit the **Fulton Mansion.** Built in 1874 by George and Harriet Fulton, this elegant mansion overlooking Aransas Bay is now a state historical park. It's within walking distance of most trailer parks, or you can drive there. Guided tours are conducted Wednesday through Sunday. But be sure to call first to make sure it will be open for your visit. Phone is (512) 729-0386.

You'll find the **Texas Maritime Museum** in Rockport at 1202 Navigation Circle, where you'll enjoy exhibits of Texas's seagoing history from Spanish galleons to modern-day oil exploration in the Gulf. Did you know that the Texas navy fought against the Mexican navy in the Texas War of Independence? For more information, telephone (512) 729-1271. If you stop at the Chamber of Commerce offices at 404 Broadway in Rockport, you'll be given a list of fifty-one things to see and do in this area. Worth a look. Telephone at the **Chamber of Commerce** is 1-800-242-0071 or (locally) 729-6445.

Leave the Sand Dollar RV Park by the north entrance, and you'll find yourself on Highway 35, heading north toward the **Aransas Na-tional Wildlife Refuge,** an hour's drive away. If your visit is between October and March, you should see large flocks of white geese feeding on the perfectly flat fields of this part of Texas. Although they nest near the Arctic Circle, they spend their winter months on the rice fields of sunny south Texas.

Take a driving tour of the Aransas Refuge after stopping at the **visitors' center** for orientation purposes. With a little luck you should see javelina, whitetail deer, many bird species and possibly an alligator or two.

Continue north on 35 to the little town of **Tivoli,** where you turn west on 238 and head for **Goliad.** Biggest attraction is the **Presidio la Bahia,** the most impressive fortification built by the Spaniards in what is now the United States of America. Texans fighting in their War for Independence from Mexico had two rallying cries ... "Remember the Alamo" and "Remember Goliad."

They had reason to remember Goliad. Colonel James Walker Fannin's forces surrendered in defeat at Coleto, 9 miles north of the Presidio. Their Mexican captors imprisoned them at the Presidio and said that they would be paroled to the United States. However, orders were received from the dictator Santa Ana and on Palm Sunday, March 27, 1836, the 341 Texans were marched out of the Presidio in three groups and executed, the biggest loss of life in the War for Texas Independence. The indignation and rage resulting from this despicable act was the greatest reason why Tejanos fought with such fury and probably accounted for the complete victory over Mexican forces and the eventual independence of Texas. Additionally, there was a flood of volunteers from the United States, which technically was an ally of Mexico and could not formally take action as a nation.

Unlike the Alamo—the fortress that became a mission, the mission that became a shrine—the Presidio at Goliad was never a mission, but was strictly a fortress. The beautiful little chapel built inside of the defensive walls was intended for the use of the Spanish soldiers stationed there and the Spanish settlers living nearby. The role of ministering to the Native American converts to Catholicism was given to the missions of Refugio, Rosario and Espiritu Santo. Be sure to visit the chapel to see the beautiful fresco at the back of the altar, and the statue of Our Lady of Loreto, which was done by Lincoln Borglum of Mt. Rushmore fame. This chapel is perhaps the most historic place in all of Texas. The first declaration of Texan Independence was signed in this chapel; this is where Fannin's men

were kept before their execution. It has been used for religious ceremonies continuously for centuries.

Further information about the Presidio can be obtained by writing to Presidio la Bahia, P.O. Box 57, Goliad, TX 77963, or by calling (512) 645-3752. Admission to the Presidio costs $3 for adults and $1 for children.

After visiting the Presidio, take time to visit the home of General Zaragosa. Born in Goliad, educated in Mexico City, Ignacio Zaragosa entered the Mexican army and rose to the rank of general. He was in charge of the Mexican army which defeated French forces at Puebla, Mexico, on May 5, 1862. It is this victory that Mexicans now celebrate as Cinco de Mayo.

There is much more to Goliad than the historic Presidio, and you should take the tour of downtown Goliad, savoring the architecture of Goliad's history. If you start at the **Chamber of Commerce,** you can pick up a leaflet that serves as guide to the walking tour. Be sure to see the blacksmith shop that features hundreds of Texas cattle brands burned into the woodworking. Visit the Hanging Tree, the Market House Museum, the Baptist Oak Tree, the famous Battlefield site where Fannin surrendered after a day and a half of fighting superior Mexican forces. Enjoy your picnic lunch at **Goliad**

State Historical Park and check out the camping possibilities in Coleto State Park. You may want to extend your stay for the fishing opportunity at this state park. RV parking is available at Coleto Creek Park, (512) 575-6366, and Goliad State Historical Park, (512) 645-3405.

After you have seen Goliad, it is time to complete the circle by heading back to San Antonio. The same Highway 238 that brought you to Goliad will take you to the Alamo City.

We've highlighted one small trip through Texas, there are thousands more. Take your time going through the magnificent empire of Texas, and you'll find much to enjoy. One word of caution: Never ask a man if he is from Texas. If he is, he'll tell you and if he isn't, why embarrass him?

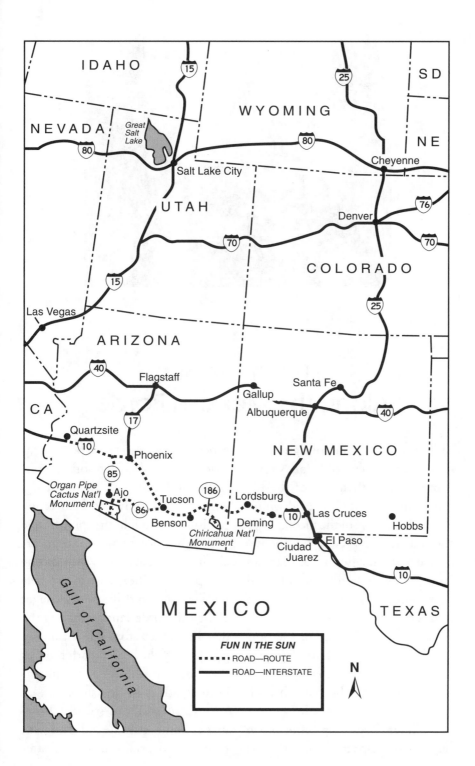

8
Fun in the Sun
Along the Mexican Border

More than half of the contiguous 48 states experience cold and snowy winters. More than half of the RV owners live in that same cold winter wonderland. One of the nicest things about owning an RV is that the RV provides the magic carpet that can take you away from that cold and snow—free as a bird to migrate to warmer climates. The magic "borderland" on both sides of the border between our country and Mexico is the favorite escape target of snowbirds heading south each winter.

Winter RV escapes come in two varieties—cheap and expensive. The expensive way is to rent a permanent space in a posh RV resort in sunshine land and park there for the winter. This allows you to enjoy poolside cocktail hours, play bridge with other northerners and generally just vegetate in the warmth. The cheap way—"inexpensive" is a better word—is to drive in easy stages along this borderland, sampling the delights of each stop. The cheap way gets you off the beaten path most of the time, but features a very much-beaten path as its first stop.

We suggest you spend Christmas at home with the kids and with relatives—the traditional way. After

New Year's Day, set out for the big "Q," **Quartzite, Arizona.** What's to see there? Must be something since about 20,000 RVs make it their home from January 1 well into February. Quartzite is located alongside U.S. Highway 10 in Arizona, but just 20 miles east of **Blythe, California.** Don't worry, you won't miss it, for the RVs are everywhere. There are trailer parks in and near Quartzite, but most of the huge assemblage of RVs simply park on land controlled by the Bureau of Land Management, where signs urge you to park at least 600 feet from the road. There's a lot of open space out here in the Arizona desert.

There are a couple of small stores that cater to the RVers, a few fast food restaurants—McDonalds is the favorite spot for coffee and conversation—and an endless sea of flea market stalls. The long lines of flea market vendors are interrupted by makeshift theaters—sometimes just straw bales to sit on and a raised platform for the performers. Country music is the main attraction here, and the nomadic residents seem to know some unwritten performance schedule, because there is always an audience for the performers, who are warmly applauded. Most of these performers offer cassette tapes of their best songs and sales are brisk.

Rock and mineral collectors congregate here in great numbers and sales and trading go on all through the season. This is the only place where I've seen a 1,000-pound block of rose quartz offered for sale—in one piece. Surprisingly, that huge chunk of beautiful rock came from South Dakota and was sold to a Texan who told me that he intended to put it in his front yard. "Don't believe I'll have to worry none about thieves carrying it off," he joked. It took a big crane and a huge flatbed truck to tote it away.

I always tell myself that I'm going to resist the wares on display here, but every time I come away with something—usually an old tool from pioneer days I'll never use. But it's great fun to stroll along the lanes and see what's offered—from wood planes of the 1800s to modern socket wrench sets, proudly stamped "made in Taiwan," from sweaters to drill presses, from rock collections to books about mushrooms.

Outside of the commercial campgrounds, usually packed to capacity, there are no hookups. However, it is possible to fill up with potable water for a $2 charge, and the county provides a dump station that does a brisk business.

It's hard to figure out the big attraction of Quartzite, whether it's the fun of visiting with other RVers from all over the nation, the country music, the rock hound business or just the irresistible lure of searching the flea markets for hidden treasures. In any event, you're never alone at Quartzite in January. You can stay a day or two, or pass the entire months of January and February in the warm sunshine.

Next, we suggest you drive eastward along the "super slab" to **Gila Bend, Arizona,** where you'll turn south on Highway 85, pass through the tiny town of **Ajo** then continue on to the **Organ Pipe Cactus National Monument.** Here the National Park Service offers 208 gravel sites, most of them wide and roomy. No hookups, but a dump site and rest rooms are available. This is a Golden Age Passport area. You are now on the Mexican border, or very

Organ Pipe Cactus National Monument is about as close to desert Mexico as you can get and still be in Arizona.

near it, and the sunshine is excellent. There's a fourteen-day limit on your stay here, and no reservations are accepted—so arrive before noon to make sure of getting a space. Sometimes you have to wait until another rig leaves and then grab that space.

A short loop road will show you most of the attractions of the monument, and if you're ambitious, there are several walking trails. The trails are rugged, however, and you'll need to wear good sturdy shoes and to carry drinking water with you—yes, even in January. Bird-watchers enjoy the monument and the chance to see many species commonly thought of as "Mexican Zone" birds that often stray this far north.

For more information about Organ Pipe Cactus National Monument, call (520) 387-6849. The National Monument is a welcome change after the hustle and bustle of Quartzite—kick back and relax!

Your next stop will be **Tucson,** and we suggest that you take Highway 86 eastward across the **Papago Indian Reservation** to give you a look at the barren desert that the Papagos call home. Maybe you'll be lucky enough to visit the Papago after a rain, when the desert explodes with beautiful flowers. Drive back northward from Organ Pipe to the aptly named village of **Why, Arizona,** and turn eastward on Highway 86. It might be a good idea to top off your gas tanks at Ajo before you tackle the Papago. You'll hardly notice the towns shown on your road map, but never fear, you'll come out at Tucson!

If you can find space there, the **City of Tucson Mountain Park** offers a very interesting spot, where two species of quail will walk past your campsite every morning, where roadrunners scrounge for bits of food around the trailers, where coyotes yodel their evening song as soon as the sun goes down. If unable to find a campsite in the big park, there are lots of good commercial campgrounds in and around Tucson.

We've enjoyed our stays at **Cactus Country RV Park.** Leave Interstate 10 at exit 275 and follow the signs. This is an excellent, modern park with lots of hookups, 246 of them at last count. Their electricity will power air conditioners and you may need that appliance, even in January. Rates are $25 for full hookups. They offer a 10 percent discount if you are a member of the Good Sam Club. The telephone number is 1-800-777-8799.

Western Way RV Resort is just one more of a dozen excellent campgrounds in the Tucson area. It is 7 or 8 miles from downtown Tucson, right on the road to **Saguaro National Monument, "Old Tucson"** and the **Desert Museum.** It offers 300 campsites, but remember that this is a popular destination during the winter and all 300 sites may be filled. Phone is (520) 578-1715; rates are $23.40 if you a member of the Good Sam Club and $26 if you are not. Usually this park is filled with retired full-timers.

There are more than one hundred trailer parks in the Tucson area, but it's a good idea to call ahead for reservations, or at least arrive early in the day so you can find a space without too much hunting. Here are the names and phone numbers of some representative trailer parks so that you can make reservations.

Tucson Mountain RV Park: (520) 883-4485
Wishing Well RV Park: (520) 825-3361
Justins RV Park: (520) 883-8340
Pima/Swan RV Park: (520) 881-4022

What's the attraction in Tucson other than sunshine and cloudless skies?

You must see the **Arizona-Sonora Desert Museum,** one of the world's best in its class! Well worth the $8.95 entry fee. (520) 883-1380.

International Wildlife Museum showcases worldwide wildlife specimens, also wildlife films shown hourly, along with guided tours. Entry fee is $6 for adults and $2 for children. (520) 629-0100.

The church at San Xavier del Bac in the Tucson area of Arizona.

If you want to get all wet, this is the place. **Justins Water World** has slides, pools and an amusement park. Entry fee is $8.95. (520) 883-8340.

Old Tucson re-creates the Old West of frontier days—lots of movies have been filmed here—lots to see and do. Warning: The access from Speedway is prohibited to trailers, so ask a few questions before you set out. (520) 883-0100.

Pima Air Museum offers excellent exhibits of aviation history, including 135 different aircraft on display. (520) 574-0462. There is a $7.50 entry fee for adults and $4 for children.

Saguaro National Monument is divided into two halves, and both are worth seeing. There are wonderful exhibits of cacti, including the giant saguaros—increasingly rare as more and more of the desert is developed into homesites and shopping centers. The monument also features exhibits, nature walks and talks by naturalists. This is a Golden Age Passport area. Call (520) 733-5100 for park information.

San Xavier Mission was started in 1783 by the Spanish padres who brought Christianity to this area. Well worth a visit, it features historical displays and lectures. No entry fee is required, although donations are gladly accepted. (520) 294-2624.

And if you're the type that prefers to shop till you drop, there's the **VF Factory Outlet** featuring clothing, luggage, household goods and much more. (520) 889-4400.

After you've had your fill of Tucson and the surrounding country, just harness up and head east on the "super slab," Interstate 10.

East of **Benson**, your Arizona highway map will call attention to several attractions, such as the **Cochise Stronghold, Tombstone Courthouse State Historic Park, Chiricahua National Monument** and **Fort Bowie National Historic Site.** Then the Interstate goes through a rocky pass (on excellent divided highway), and you are in the Land of Enchantment—New Mexico. Just 3 miles east of the border, turn off and visit **Steins** (pronounced *Steens*) named for a commanding officer of the U.S. Dragoons who camped here during the Civil War. As many as 1,000 people called Steins home in those days, when it was a stop on the famed Butterfield Stage route, but today only the rather junky remains of the small town remain.

Steins had one big strike against it as an "up-and-coming" town. There was no water available, and during its heyday, Steins paid a dollar a barrel for water hauled there from **Doubtful Canyon.** That was back when many a man worked eight hours and earned 25¢.

They claim that Doubtful Canyon got its name because it was doubtful that the stage would get through the canyon without being robbed. When the Civil War got going, the Congress closed the Butterfield Trail by order. Defiantly, one last stage left **Mesilla** (south of **Las Cruces**) and headed for Tucson. That stage was ambushed near Steins and all the passengers were killed. A minimal fee is charged for a tour of the place. (505) 542-9791.

You can headquarter in **Lordsburg,** where there are many campgrounds and motels. If you do stop there, you'll be on the doorstep of another, more interesting ghost town—incongruously named **Shakespeare.**

This ghost town has a fabulous story to tell. It began with a silver strike and a diamond swindle in 1870. Under the name of Ralston City it prospered and grew to 3,000 people. In 1879, residents decided

to "culture" their raw town, so they named it "Shakespeare." In 1893, an economic depression killed its mining business and the town died. Nobody lived there for a while, then two desperadoes named Russian Bill and Sandy King made it their headquarters. A posse from nearby Lordsburg surprised the two one sunny day and hung them from the rafters of the little restaurant that was still in operation in Shakespeare.

The next morning the stage stopped there for breakfast. They found the two bodies still hanging. Legend has it that they cut them down, hauled them away and then enjoyed breakfast. There was another mining boom from 1908 to 1932, and Shakespeare again prospered—in a lawless way, with lots of hangings.

Since 1935, the Hill family has owned the place and trespassers are not welcome! Do *not* try to visit Shakespeare on your own; it won't work! Tours of the place are conducted on two weekends each month, however, during tourist season, along with a series of re-enactments of historic events. For information about Shakespeare, contact the Lordsburg Chamber of Commerce, or write directly to Shakespeare Ghost Town, P.O. Box 253, Lordsburg, NM 88045.

Camping is inexpensive in Lordsburg, with a fine **KOA** charging $17.50 per night for full hookup and $16.50 for electric only; call (505) 542-8003. **Chaparral Trailer Park** offers sites as low as $8 ($9 with cable). Phone is (505) 542-9814. Lordsburg is an important stop on the railroad going east and west through this flat land, and campground noise is often high as a result of being located near both a busy railroad and a busy highway. Same thing is true of the campgrounds at Deming, the next stop on our trip through "southwestern yesterday" country.

Make your next headquarters at **Deming,** which advertises itself as the home of clean water and fast ducks. The water is clean, and every summer Deming stages its duck races. For three years in a row the race was won by the same man—a man named (would I lie to you?) Duck. Competition is stiff, because the first prize is $7,500—but you'll be there in the wintertime, and no ducks will be racing.

Let's first find a campsite. **Sunrise RV Park,** (505) 546-8565, has 60 units and a lot of long pull throughs, rest rooms and hot showers. **Little Vineyard RV Park** has 60 units, rest rooms, hot showers and cable TV. Rates start at $12 for two people, $2 for cable TV. Phone (505) 546-3560.

If railroad and big truck noise bothers you, I have an excellent suggestion. Ask directions to the **Rock Hound State Park,** just 12 miles out of Deming on the side of a small mountain. The park offers 29 RV spaces, 22 of them with electricity. If you can park here, you've got it made. I'll guarantee you lots of space and lots of clean air to breathe. Easterners are sometimes heard remarking that "they've got air here you can't even see!" It's a good idea to phone ahead to make sure there's a space waiting for you; call (505) 546-6182.

Once camped, you'll probably spend some time taking in the immense view to the west. And if you're interested, this park lives up to its name. Exhibits display the various minerals and semi-precious gemstones found in the vicinity. It's the only state park I know of that urges you to hunt for mineral samples and then allows you to take them home. Among the gemstones found here are geodes, opals, agates, quartz crystals, perlite and pitchstone.

Contact the very active **Chamber of Commerce** at 800 East Pine in Deming and enjoy its color-coded tour guides. You'll visit the **Luna Mimbres Museum** for interesting exhibits on the ancient Native Americans of the Southwest and get a good look at the history of this town from its earliest pioneer days. They'll also help you plan your trips to two other state parks from your Deming headquarters.

A second state park to visit is **City of Rocks,** 23 miles north of Deming on U.S. 180. The turnoff to the state park is marked, but watch for it so you don't miss it. Here you'll find a very large assortment of weird rock formations, strangely beautiful. You can drive in among the rock formations, so even those of us who are couch potatoes can enjoy them. The geologists tell us that these unique shapes are made of tuff spewed out by an ancient volcano and fused together by their own weight, then carved and shaped by wind and water. There is primitive camping available here at $7 per night, with a rest room, showers and a potable water supply. I suggest staying overnight only if there's a full moon and a cloudless sky—when the weird shapes seem to come alive in the moonlight, creating their own light and shadow show. I don't recommend you hike after dark. Rattlesnakes have been seen here, as in most of the southwestern corner of New Mexico. The telephone number is (505) 536-2800.

The third state park I want you to visit is **Pancho Villa State Park** located right on the Mexican border at the small town of **Columbus.** I find it strange that we named a state park after a Mexican *bandido* who invaded the United States, shot up the small town of Columbus and then retreated into Mexico. But

Pancho Villa State Park in New Mexico commemorates the last incursion on American soil by foreign troops.

Pancho Villa is still a heroic figure to the mostly Hispanic population of this area. He twisted Uncle Sam's tail and got away with it, which makes him something special to *Mexicanos* on both sides of the border.

You can camp in a small but interesting trailer park in the park itself, flanked by rows of cacti of every size and shape imaginable. A small museum will tell you what happened here on March 9, 1916.

Pancho Villa led a ragtag army that had no legal status in Mexico. He fought against the federal armies of Mexican President Carranza. When President Woodrow Wilson recognized the Carranza government diplomatically, Pancho was insulted and angry. He led over 900 soldiers across the border in a daring nocturnal raid on **Camp Furlong,** striking at 4:15 A.M. He caught the U.S. Army asleep, of course, and most of them had to draw ammunition before they could begin to fight. After taking a swipe at Camp Furlong, Pancho's guerrillas looted stores in nearby Columbus and set fire to some of the town's buildings. About that time the U.S. Army arrived and the raid turned into a disaster for Villa's army. The raiders lost 142 men in Columbus, and another 75 were cut down as they fled back into Mexico.

If it surprises you to learn that Mexicans once invaded the United States, you're not alone. Study the exhibits in the museum housed in an abandoned railroad depot building and bring yourself up-to-date, historically. The state park is built around the ruins of Camp Furlong and you'll even find the grease rack where the American army greased their primitive trucks. A "trivia"

The Ajo Mountain drive in the Organ Pipe Monument takes the traveler through an area of rugged beauty.

point in U.S. history—this was the first time we tried to use aircraft in a war. The biplanes proved to be too flimsy and failed miserably.

After you've seen everything in Deming, and visited the three state parks—Rock Hound, City of Rocks and Pancho Villa—get back on the super slab eastbound and head for **Las Cruces,** about 65 miles east of Deming. You might want to try one of my favorite campgrounds, the **KOA** high on the hills to the west of the city, with its unparalleled view of the city lights below. You can see all the way to the fabled **Organ Mountains** far to the east.

There are many more campgrounds. Try the **Coachlight RV Park** at 301 South Motel Boulevard, (505) 526-3301. **El Patio RV Park,** 1557 Calle de Vista, (505) 524-7504. **Siesta RV Camp,** 1551 Avenida de Mesilla, costs $19.95 for two people with all hookups, (505) 523-6816. **St. John's RV Park,** 3115 El Camino Real, offers sites with full hookups for $20, (505) 526-6290.

Please visit the **Las Cruces Chamber of Commerce** at 311 Downtown Mall for information on activities for the week and to make sure you don't miss something you might really enjoy, such as NMSU basketball games and symphony concerts. This is an active city with lots of civic pride, and there is always something going on.

Las Cruces, with more than 60,000 people, is New Mexico's second largest city (Albuquerque has about half a million). But we're out for "sun and fun" without spending all of our retirement fund, so let's travel a few miles north, along the **Rio Grande** to our last hideaway from the workaday troubles of the world.

Roughly 18 miles north of Interstate 25 you'll find the signs for the turnoff to **Fort Selden State Monument** and **Leasburg Dam State Park**. Fort Selden was built in 1865 to protect early settlers from Apache raiders. The commanding officer of the fort in the 1880s was a young captain named Arthur MacArthur. You may have heard of his son, Douglas MacArthur. The future General Douglas MacArthur grew up in the adobe houses of Fort Selden, learning to ride and shoot while living here. Today there are only the crumbling adobe walls and the tall cottonwoods that once provided shade for army troops. It's fascinating to walk among these ruins and read the plaques that tell you which building housed which family. Let your imagination run wild and you'll hear again the bugle calling the troops to assembly, or perhaps the melancholy strains of "Taps." Some of the lessons learned by this young army "brat" helped

Douglas MacArthur become Supreme Commander of the Allied Forces in World War II.

When the Apaches were no longer a threat, the fort was abandoned in 1891. After a century of neglect, the fort was made a state park. A leisurely stroll along the trail leading through the ruins is a pleasant way to spend a day in the sunshine. Fort Selden doesn't have a campground, but just 2 miles away on the other side of the river lies Leasburg Dam State Park, which has an excellent campground. There are only 18 sites with electricity but many undeveloped sites. As in all of New Mexico's state parks, the camping fee is $7 without electricity and $11 with electricity. If the campground is full when you arrive, take one of the undeveloped sites and be ready to move into one of the sites with electricity the next morning as soon as someone moves out.

This trip is one of the greatest—if what you want is peace and quiet and warm sunshine. There are literally hundreds of side trips we haven't mentioned because there simply isn't enough room to tell you all about southern Arizona and New Mexico. If you're looking for an inexpensive tour far from winter snows and freezing temperatures, this is the tour for you!

ARKANSAS

LOUISIANA

MISSISSIPPI

I-20

Monroe

Vicksburg

Jackson

I-55

I-20

Mississippi River

Alexandria

I-1

Simmesport

I-49

St. Francisville

Atchafalaya River

Baton Rouge

I-12

Hammond

I-59

Lafayette

I-10

I-10

Lake Pontchartrain

New Orleans

N

Intracoastal Waterway

Morgan City

Houma

BARGING THE BAYOUS
OF LOUISIANA
•••••• ROUTE
ROAD—INTERSTATE

Gulf of Mexico

9

Barging the Bayous of Louisiana

Ray Gaines and I have been friends for a lot of years, dating back to when we both led caravans into Mexico. With his wife, Laura, Ray Gaines has been a full-timer for almost thirty years. He's also a man who gets lots of good ideas, so I wasn't surprised when he called to invite me on the first ever "Barging the Bayous" RV caravan a couple of years ago. But I *was* surprised by the trip.

Ray had definite ideas about the needs of a river craft that could carry as many as thirty-nine of the biggest RVs and transport them safely and comfortably along hundreds of miles of the Mississippi River—through swamps, the historic Atchafalaya Basin and some of the

most scenic river country in Louisiana—Cajun Country.

Ed Conrad of Compass Marine in New Orleans knew the barge business inside and out and had the know-how to translate Ray Gaines's ideas into reality. They came up with a finished barge that was 240 feet long and 50 feet wide. Put three of these barges together end to end and add the powerful tugboat that provided the power and we had a total length of just under 800 feet!

Each campsite on the barges was marked off by painted lines on deck to guide the RVs to their space. Each RV had enough room to extend its awning fully without touching its neighbor. And get this—each RV had its own hookups for electricity, water and sewer drain! And all facilities were available twenty-four hours a day. The electricity came from a big generator mounted on the stern of the last barge—just ahead of the tugboat.

That first trip was an eyeopener! The barge was moored to a wharf on a backwater right in New Orleans, a few miles from the mighty Mississippi River. Each of us drove our own vehicle to its assigned place on the barge, easily maneuvering into individual campsites. We had twenty-seven vehicles on that inaugural cruise, and it took less than two hours to jockey all the rigs into place. We extended our awnings and got out the deck chairs to enjoy the October sunshine.

The strangest part was getting used to the fact that our campground was taking us to see the sights, instead

Riding the barges, you have a ringside view of the always fascinating river traffic on the mighty Mississippi.

of the usual routine of driving to the sights then coming back to camp at the end of the day. We could truly relax and leave the driving to the skipper of the powerful tug *Lagonda*.

With the three barges securely tethered end to end, the *Lagonda* moved us westward down the **Intracoastal Waterway.** I had to look at the bank to realize that we were actually moving. There was very little sound from the tug's powerful engines, and the incredibly stable barges seemed to be anchored in cement as they floated along without any sensation of movement. It was a very peaceful way to travel, and an exciting way to see the sights of this busy waterway, which brings our country's produce to New Orleans for shipment overseas and takes incoming freight from the port of New Orleans and distributes it upriver.

The hours sped by as we went gliding up the busy waterway—but there was no time to get too relaxed; several treats were in store for us. First of all, a boat came alongside and delivered *muffelatas* on board. The *muffelata* is a whole round loaf of bread sliced in half and filled with a delicious assortment of seafood swimming in a savory, distinctively "N'Awluns" sauce. If you've never eaten Cajun cuisine, you've never really eaten.

Late in the afternoon, we docked at **Houma** and were welcomed by civic authorities greeting this inaugural cruise. After the brief visit, we silently moved another 21 miles up the Intracoastal and tied up to the bank for the night. I was already asleep and didn't watch the mooring procedure.

The second day started out in fine style, with the tour company furnishing breakfast, delivered on board by a very versatile Cajun named Ron Guidry. After catering an excellent breakfast of hotcakes and sausage with all the trimmings, he took half of our group at a time in his pontoon boat, driving deep into the beautiful and trackless Atchafalaya Swamp. More than a guide, he turned out to be a locally famous entertainer who could call up alligators to feed on chicken fat. Honest—we all took pictures of the big 'gator leaping nearly all the way out of the water to snatch the offered bait. Then Ron picked up a guitar and started singing a selection of entertaining Cajun songs, ending up with his own composition, "Mud Bug Boogie." He was living proof that Cajuns are fun-loving people who know how to have a good time.

About 4:00 that afternoon, we moored to the bank in **Morgan City,** where we were warmly welcomed and given a tour of the city in private RVs driven by their owners. The tour ended at a local park where we were serenaded by a band and entertained

by a troupe of youthful dancers. When the performance ended, we moved upstream to moor for the night.

On the third day we got underway at 4:00 A.M., but I slept until after seven, oblivious to the fact that we were already moving. We enjoyed a placid day until about 4:00 that afternoon—then it was time to jamboree!

We tied up to the bank at **Whiskey Bay** and rode company-furnished buses to **McGee's Landing.** We feasted on deep-fried catfish and crab cakes along with other spicy Cajun treats. Local dance experts showed us how to dance "bayou style," and the foot-stomping fun continued late into the night. Then we were bused back to our quiet campground—not on the riverbank, but on the river.

The fourth day started with a real gullywasher of a rainstorm. It poured for about ten minutes, then the sun came out and we moved upstream to the swing bridge at **Krotz Springs,** where repairs had to be made to the bridge before they could swing it out of our way. Once past this obstacle, we had another deluge for twenty minutes, a deluge that tested the water tightness of every RV. By the time the rain had passed, we were leaving the Atchafalaya River and moving into the **Red River.** By midafternoon, we'd entered the mighty Father of Waters itself and were moored to a Mississippi bank for a potluck dinner—

the wagonmaster furnished more than enough baked ham for everyone, and each rig contributed a dish. Needless to say, we ate well!

The fifth day produced new surprises. We had run downriver to milepost 261 where we tied up to transfer to air-conditioned buses for a wonderful day-long tour of antebellum plantation homes near **St. Francesville.** After touring the first mansion—Greenwood—the buses took us out to lunch at The Inn before going on to visit two more elegant pre–Civil War homes, The Myrtles and Rosedown. We were given plenty of time to thoroughly examine these reminders of a lifestyle of long ago. Back on board our peripatetic playground, we sat under the awnings and watched the white-tailed deer drinking at the beautiful banks of the big river. Before dark, the barges were moored in a quiet backwater for the night.

The sixth day brought us to a city dock in **Baton Rouge** near the **Maritime Museum** and the **USS Kidd,** a World War II destroyer, both of which we toured on company-provided tickets. That afternoon we enjoyed an ice cream social as our campground glided down the Mississippi River. Travel continued that day until almost midnight, and we sat on deck to watch the fascinating, constantly changing parade of river craft, lit by a full moon.

The seventh day's start was delayed for two reasons—a heavy fog and a French toast and sausage breakfast put on by our hosts, the wagon-master team of Vic and Helen McWhirter. As it was Sunday, Helen McWhirter led a nondenominational service that was well attended. By midafternoon, we were approaching New Orleans. We had a riverman's view of this most fascinating city as we moved in to dock at the very foot of the famed **River Walk,** just two blocks from the New Orleans Hilton and within easy walking distance of the French Quarter. We went ashore at about 4:00 P.M. led by the high-stepping strutter who calls himself Napoleon, whose parade ended up at tables full of gumbo and dessert to ensure that we received an authentic "N'Awluns" welcome.

After our welcoming food, Ray Gaines distributed three-day passes for riding the streetcars and buses of the city, as well as a ticket good for a horse-drawn carriage ride through the French Quarter. We spent that evening "cruising" the famed **Vieux Carré** (French Quarter)—and we had better accommodations than those tourists paying $160 per day in the nearby hotels.

On the eighth day we enjoyed a group tour by bus to see the sights of this fascinating city. The tour guide was very knowledgeable and added much to our enjoyment of the two-and-a-half-hour trip. The rest of the day was spent at leisure, giving us time to sample more of the wonderful cuisine of the Crescent City. It's fun to drink café au lait at the **Cafe du Mond** and eat the deliciously sweet *beignets*. After admiring the work of the artists displaying their wares in **Jackson's Square**, I must confess to eating another *muffelata* at **Cafe Maspero.**

The ninth day was also "at leisure," but there's so much to do that the time seemed to fly by. You could take your choice—Pete Fountain and Al Hirt were playing in the Vieux Carré. And if you got in line early enough, it was possible to buy tickets to the world-famous **Preservation Hall** to hear the timeless music of New Orleans jazz as it should be heard, played the way Louis Armstrong played it—and Big Jim Robinson, Sweet Emma Barret, the Humphrey Brothers, Cie Frazier and Slow Drag Pavageau.

On the tenth and final day of our trip, we moved away from the River Walk mooring maneuvering through the locks into the Intracoastal Waterway and back to our embarkation point. Driving off the barges was easier than driving on, and we returned to the normal world after nine days of living a fantasy.

Best of all, we hadn't used a single gallon of gasoline, our fresh-

Your own chartered buses will take you to tour the antebellum homes, with plenty of time allowed to really look at these beautiful estates.

water tanks were full and our wastewater tanks were empty.

From that first trip several years ago, Ray Gaines has continued to expand the operation and now offers barge tours of the **Tennessee-Tombigbee waterway,** ten-day cruises through **Acadiana,** nine-day Fall Festival cruises that run through **Guntersville, Alabama,** and **Chattanooga, Tennessee,** and fifteen-day cruises on "three terrific rivers."

Prices for these barge trips run from $2,100 per rig and two people all the way up to $4,900 for the longest tours. Each tour includes more than just the barge trip, so you have a wide assortment of fun trips to choose from. You can get full information and descriptive literature by calling 1-800-256-6100. I guarantee you won't get tired of driving your rig on the barge trip, and you'll sure save a lot of money on gas.

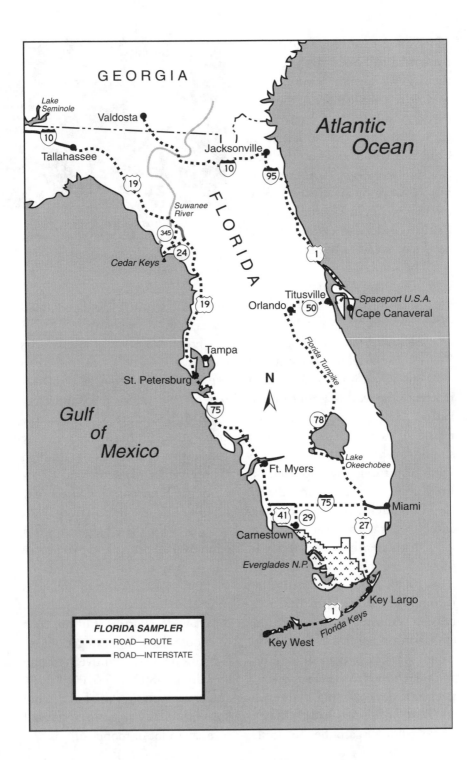

10
A Florida Sampler

For a great number of North Americans—both from the United States and Canada—Florida is the winter destination of choice. This isn't surprising. Florida has much to offer in the wintertime—winter up north, that is, since Florida seldom sees any real winter weather.

Before getting into particulars, let's get a few facts straight. First, Florida is a very big state. When we entered from Alabama, we asked how far it was to Tallahassee, the state capital. The answer took us by surprise: 200 miles. When we added in the 616 miles from Tallahassee to Key West, we decided that this was a very long state, indeed, although its total area doesn't come close to that of Alaska, Texas, California, Montana or New Mexico.

Second, the weather is definitely not the same in all parts of Florida. On our last January-February excursion to the sunshine state, we experienced cold winds and rains in the St. Augustine area up north. At the same time, most of central Florida was warm and sunny, while winds and rain once again held sway over the Keys and all the area south of Miami. For the most part, the weather is better the farther south you go.

Third, Florida offers an excellent highway system, with broad-laned divided main roads, most secondary roads hard-surfaced and no hills or mountains at all. Florida is flat as a pancake over 99 percent of its area.

Fourth, Florida has literally tens of thousands of trailer parks, some good, some excellent, a very few less than desirable. Although advance reservations are usually a good idea, you won't need to worry about finding a space for the night. This isn't always true in the Keys, where space is very limited. There it's a good idea to make reservations several days in advance.

Whether your main interest is wildlife, sandy beaches, attractions such as Disney World or the Cypress Gardens water skiers, deep-sea fishing offshore, flea markets or historic places, you'll never exhaust all the possibilities in any six months. Since we can't tell you *all* about Florida and its attractions, we'll simply present a "sampler" of places to stay, things to do and places to see. We make no claim to listing everything—we're just going to tell you what we did recently.

It's a long drive from our Albuquerque home to Florida so we pulled into the KOA west of the state capital. It's called the **Chattahoochee/Tallahassee KOA** because it isn't really close to either town. It's clean and very quiet, and we enjoyed resting up in the shady park. Then we visited the **Florida Camping Association** offices in Tallahassee and picked up a list of its members, along with a list of state parks for future reference. Florida has many state parks, only a small percentage of which allow camping.

We made the state park in **Cedar Key** our first destination. This small park has only 30 spaces, so we were glad we called ahead and got their last available spot. It's on the Gulf of Mexico side of the peninsula and easy to find on your highway map. At 12 feet above sea level, the camp is at the highest point on Cedar Key. In addition to its oceanfront location, the park is within easy walking distance of almost anything you'd want to see in Cedar Key. Walk to the downtown area for curio shopping and to the beachside restaurants. We tried several and settled on the **Sea Breeze on the Dock** restaurant, (352) 543-5738. Elida enjoyed the crab Florentine and I had the seafood platter of fish, oysters, shrimp and scallops, all delicious.

Ocean fishing is good here and charters can be arranged with Captain Ron Vaught at (352) 543-5625, or with Captain Dick Brown at (352) 543-5322. Grouper, king mackerel and the many members of the snapper family can be taken and all provide tasty meals. Boat rides are also available aboard the *Island Hopper*, P.O. Box 106, Cedar Key, FL 32625, (352) 543-5904.

Cost is $10 per adult and $5 for children.

Sightseeing trips can take you to the **Lower Suwanee National Wildlife Refuge** and to the **Cedar Key Museum,** which is just about 2 $^1/_2$ miles from the campground. Admission to the museum is only $1. This little city was once the boomtown that produced the cedar "penny pencils" we oldsters remember from our early school days. Most of the cedar came from this area, hence the name. The cedar was over-harvested and this killed the goose that laid the golden egg. Changes in maritime shipping with bigger and "deeper" vessels made the shallow-water port obsolete, and Cedar Key is now only a tiny remnant of what it once was. The one constant through the centuries has been the fishing industry, which is still very important here in Cedar Key. Sport fishing is allowed right from the pier at this park. The beautiful sunsets seen from this park are worth far more than the $10 daily camping fee, which is a real bargain. If you just can't live without cable TV, it's $2 a day additional. But call ahead, for this is a very small park.

Leaving Cedar Key, we traveled slowly south to **Homosassa Springs State Wildlife Park,** home to a wonderful assortment of wildlife, featuring one of the world's rarest and most endangered mammals, the

An adult brown pelican poses for the camera at Flamingo in Everglades National Park.

manatee. These almost shapeless half-ton mammals cannot live out of water. They swim slowly and languidly and devour green vegetation at a phenomenal rate. You'll get to see them up close—as close as 5 feet—when you go down into the underwater rooms with glass walls that give you a good view. The early sailors who first saw the manatees said that they looked like beautiful women, like mermaids. After you've seen them up close, you'll agree that those sailors must have been away from home too long. There are also alligators that come in response to the feeding bell, allowing splendid photo opportunities. For the bird-watchers, many free-flying species of birds have become very tame here where they know they are safe and will usually pose for photographs at close range. Those interested in fishing will find themselves drooling at the sight of hundreds of jack crevalle—a saltwater species that comes up into freshwater and is known for its sporting qualities as a fighter with stamina.

Want to learn the real difference between alligators and crocodiles? This is the place to study both species. There is also a lovely pontoon boat tour back into the swamps, adding another excellent opportunity for bird photography. The boat tour is included in the price of admission, which totals $11.79 for two people. For further information about Homosassa State Park, write

One of the main buildings at Koreshan State Historic Site, near Estero, Florida.

to Homosassa State Wildlife Park, 9225 West Fishbowl Drive, Homosassa Springs, FL 32646.

Heading on south, we ran into a horrendous traffic jam on Highway 19 just north of **St. Petersburg.** We solved that problem by getting off the main drag and working our way over to a pleasant **KOA** in St. Petersburg. Morning traffic was much easier to negotiate, and we took our time getting a good look at the St. Petersburg area.

Incidentally, St. Petersburg boasts of being the sunniest place in the world—with the most days of sunlight. It lived up to that reputation when we visited. But we decided that we didn't come to Florida to look at cities, and we exited on the road that crosses the long suspension bridge on the way to **Bradenton** and **Sarasota.** Ringling Brothers, Barnum and Bailey Circus spends its off-season in Sarasota, and it's worth your while to make inquiries—you just might get to see the circus.

Just a little ways off of southbound Highways 19 and 41, we saw the signs leading to **Koreshan State Historic Site** and went in for a look. We found a fabulous thing—an attempt at establishing the City of God on earth. A New York doctor named Cyrus Teed believed that he was "illuminated" by God and he established Koreshan here at the city of **Estero.** His idyllic settlement was based on celibacy, which would seem to me to doom the idea from the start. His settlement still displays the Founder's House, a bakery, a planetary court, the art hall and the fine Scrub Oak Camping area.

Central to the Koreshan belief was the idea that the earth was hollow and that humans lived on the inside of the earth, with the sun, moon and planets hanging in the hollow center of the earth. Don't laugh too loudly, for he offered a prize of $10,000 to anyone who could prove that he was wrong. No one was able to claim the prize. Although Dr. Teed believed he was immortal, he died at the age of 69. His settlement started to lose members soon thereafter, and in 1961 the four remaining members of the settlement deeded it to the Florida parks in memory of Dr. Teed. If you want to learn more, write to Koreshan Historic Site, P.O. Box 7, Estero, FL, 33928. It is possible to reserve camping here, and it's a nice place to headquarter while you walk the trails of Koreshan itself.

Our next stop was at the **KOA at Naples/Marco Island.** This very large park is an attraction in itself and one of the finest trailer parks I've ever visited. We stayed a couple of days longer than we had planned, as I especially enjoyed both the swimming pool and the hot tub.

Next stop was at **Everglades City,** which is about as big a change as you can imagine. We found **Barrons RV Park,** (941) 695-3331, checked in and then went sight-seeing. Other possibilities are **Big Cypress Trail Campground,** (941) 695-2275, **Chokoloskee Island Park,** (941) 695-2414 and **Glades Haven RV Park,** (941) 695-2746.

First stop was at the National Park concessionaire, which operates boat tours in the brackish waters of the north end of the **Everglades National Park.** The very interesting tour costs $10 per person and is worth much more. The knowledgeable boat operator had keen eyes for the birds and animals and called our attention to ospreys, oyster catchers, skimmers, great white herons, southern bald eagles, Everglades kites, black vultures, wood storks, purple gallinule, ibises, roseate spoonbills and manatees (in the wild state) that are easy to see but hard to photograph, as they are 95 percent submerged in the muddy waters. As a special bonus, a school of playful bottle-nosed dolphins frolicked around our boat. For more information about Everglades National Park, write to P.O. Box 279, Homestead, FL 33034, or call (305) 242-7700.

Fishing is good in these waters, and we saw many private boats enjoying the lovely weather and calm

Take the tour boat at Everglades City to see much wildlife. If you're serious about photography, take a position on the upper deck to get the best angles for bird photos.

water. **Fishing guides** are available for hire, including Tony Brock at (941) 695-4150, Bob Chipman at (941) 695-2258, Max Miller at (941) 695-2420 and Cecil Oglesby at (941) 695-2910.

After the boat tour, we drove further south to **Chokoloskee** and found several more commercial campgrounds there. We ate our evening meal at the Oyster House right on the main drag of tiny Everglades City and it was good; (305) 695-2073.

Many operators offer exciting **air boat tours** of this part of the "glades." We recommend Wooten's Air Boat Tours, because they give a longer run and go deeper into the glades. Their phone number is (941) 695-2781. Do you consider yourself too old for such a daring ride?

C'mon, live a little; it's perfectly safe.

For those who are fascinated by the endless river of grass that is the Everglades, there are canoe trails for your use and places to rent canoes. If you're really daring, there's a 40- to 50-mile-long canoe trail from Everglades City all the way down to **Flamingo** at the extreme south end of the giant park.

Leaving Everglades City on the **Tamiami Trail**—often called Alligator Alley—we round a series of six primitive campgrounds along the trail. Next trip we'll save a couple of nights' camping fees and enjoy the company of kindred souls staying there. All of these campgrounds were in use, but there was plenty of space for additional campers.

It's only about 130 miles from Everglades City to **Flamingo** at the south end of the park, where we checked into the primitive campgrounds provided by the National Park Service. Be sure you have your Golden Age Passport with you, because it gives you free entry to the national park and also gives you 50 percent off the $8 camping fee. Four bucks a night is a bargain for anyone's budget, and the campground is spacious, quiet and very nice. One thing to remember is that here you will definitely need mosquito repellent if you plan on taking one of the interpretative nature trails or going boating.

For the ambitious canoeist, this is the southern terminus of the canoe trail we mentioned at Everglades City. For the less ambitious, there's a good boat tour of the fascinating, island-studded **Florida Bay.** Cost is $11 for adults and $6 for children. There is an interesting visitor center at Flamingo and a fine restaurant. This campground can be the focus of an energetic visit, or it can be the most peaceful, restful spot in Florida—it's all up to you. But remember that you only paid $4 per night because tomorrow you'll be in Key West.

The southernmost city in the United States, **Key West** is a fascinating place, but definitely expensive. There's very little dirt here to build on, so real estate is valuable. We paid $35 per night for a space with very small sites and lots of crowds. This was at **Boyd's Campground,** right on the beach. There's a bus that comes to the entrance of the campground every half hour (more or less) and for 75¢ it will take you to the downtown area by a very circuitous route that gives you a fine tour of the fascinating city. If you make your reservation early enough, you may be able to get a beachfront site, where your back window will face the water. Boyd's address is 6401 Maloney Avenue, Key West, FL 33040, (305) 294-1465.

Once downtown, you can take the **Conch Train tour,** which costs $14 per person and is probably the best way to get an overview of this historic and picturesque old town. From the train tour, you can visit the historic **Hemingway House** for $6 a person. As an aspiring writer, the Hemingway House was practically a shrine for me. I looked at the desk where Hemingway wrote most of his published novels and laughed at the story about the urinal at Sloppy Joe's cantina where Hemingway did his drinking. Hemingway claimed that he had title to the urinal because "most of my income has gone through it." When he was in Europe during the Spanish Civil War, his wife had a huge swimming pool excavated out of the coral limestone that forms Key West. It cost some $40,000, more than Hemingway had paid for the entire estate a few years earlier. He is reported to have said, "You've spent all of my money right down to the last penny," and tossed his "last" red cent to the floor. This story is perpetuated by the penny permanently installed on the floor. Hemingway wasn't the only well-known writer to call Key West home; Robert Frost and Tennessee Williams also lived and worked here.

You can also spend the day just walking around the historic district, strolling to the dock area where the charter boats are located. You can always find a fishing trip to suit your needs. And if you don't want to catch fish, but prefer simply to look at them, take a tour on the **MV** *Discovery,* a glass-bottom boat, (305) 293-0099. Consider a visit to the **Fort Zachary Taylor Historic Site,** or even a long boat ride out to the **Dry Tortugas** where Uncle Sam maintains the **Fort Jefferson Historic Site.**

The **Audubon House and Gardens** can be visited on the Conch Train tour. It is located at the intersection of Whitehead and Greene Streets, (305) 294-2116. The big luxurious house was built by Captain John J. Geiger, a harbor pilot and master salvager. He furnished the house with treasures from wrecked ships. His family lived in it for more than one hundred and twenty years. Famed artist John James Audubon lived in Key West while he studied the birds of the Keys and did much of his bird painting. The Wolfson family restored the house and stocked it with Audubon memorabilia, which makes it a very interesting stop. It is currently administered by the Florida Audubon Society.

President Harry Truman loved Key West and called it the Little White House. In 1949, he wrote to his wife Bess, "I've a notion to move the capital to Key West and just stay."

Key West is right out in the sea, so seafood is fresh and delicious. It is also more expensive than the same seafood found in your hometown. Key West is fascinating, but bring your wallet and credit cards.

Returning to the mainland, you'll enjoy vistas of sea and sky and the islands that form this magical chain. You'll also see signs for a seafood restaurant named **The Green Turtle.** Read the signs and watch for this spot. Don't arrive before noon, because that's when they open. They served us the finest seafood we had on the entire Florida trip and at very reasonable prices. Don't miss this one.

Coming off the Keys, we headed for the **Clewiston KOA,** at the south end of huge **Okeechobee Lake,** one of the most famous black bass fishing spots in the world. This is a nice campground with a very friendly atmosphere (ask the owner-manager, Stuart, to tell you the Cajun story about the "four doors.") You'll find many bass fishermen at the KOA, and like anglers everywhere, they'll be glad to advise you. In addition to the KOA, there is an RV park owned by the world famous bass fisherman, Roland Martin, right on the launching ramp that leads into Okeechobee. While you're in the Clewiston area, be sure to eat at **Robbie's Restaurant,** on the main street in Clewiston. The menu is simple, but you get large portions of tasty food, with lots of ambiance. The locals eat here, especially at noon. Better get there before the clock strikes twelve, or you'll have to wait. If having breakfast, we recommend a "2 by 4."

Our next stop was **Fort Wilderness** on the grounds of **Disney World** in **Orlando.** This place is so famous that I need not beat the drums for Walt Disney's place. This is a near perfect campground, with lots of space, lots of privacy and all hookups, of course. You walk a city block to where the touring bus picks you up. The bus takes you to the monorail that delivers you right to the door of **Epcot Center** or whatever part of Disney World you want to see first. To my mind this is the single greatest attraction in Florida, equally interesting to young and old. But you can't just drive in and expect to get a RV space at Fort Wilderness. Everything is done by advance reservation, so see your travel agent for a package that includes both the campground and Disney World attractions. The Fort Wilderness dates will be set in concrete, and you'll have to adjust the rest of your Florida trip to fit, but no one in his or her right mind would visit Florida and not see Disney World. Touring Disney World can be strenuous for us oldsters, so I offer a suggestion— buy tickets for Monday, Wednesday and Friday. Use Tuesday and Thurs-

day to rest up between the long days of touring, which involves lots of standing in line.

Camping at Fort Wilderness is an attraction in itself; many come here and camp for a few days and don't even go to Disney World. Fort Wilderness covers 740 acres. The park totals 830 spaces, and they're almost always filled, so go the reservation route. For further information dial 1-800-W-Disney. If you can't get into Fort Wilderness, there are many good trailer parks offering free shuttle bus service to and from Disney World. For example, there are two of **Raccoon Lake Camp Resort,** one on U.S. 192, west of Disney World and another on Interstate 4 and 482; both can be reached at 1-800-776-YOGI. Their rates are $32 per night with full hookups, and reservations can be made years in advance.

In the Orlando area there are many other attractions, and one of the best is **Sea World,** an Anheuser-Busch theme park. Located at the intersection of Interstate 4 and SR 528, it is easily reached. Plan on spending the entire day there, for there is much to see and do. The park opens every morning at 9:00, 365 days a year. Major credit cards are accepted—except American Express.

After Disney World, we headed for another wonderful entertainment—**Cypress Gardens.** Plan on spending an entire day there. We camped at the **Hammondell Campground** just a few miles from the huge parking lot at Cypress Gardens. It costs $20 per person but is worth it. Not only will you see the greatest waterskiing show on earth (you won't believe your eyes), you'll also get a lot of laughs at the Feathered Follies. Ever hear a parrot trained to belch realistically on command? Other parts of the act, featuring five different kinds of parrots, are more refined. The show certainly raised my opinion of parrot intelligence. You'll also see the world's greatest collection of butterflies, both mounted and very much alive, and walk through the restored buildings of an elegant southern plantation. Excellent gift shops are scattered throughout the premises. Cypress Gardens—a fine stop on our Florida Sampler.

Our next stop will be headquarters for a visit to America's "space coast." You have lots of choices for your headquarters, but here are two good ones: **The Great Outdoors,** located just half a mile west of Interstate 95 on SR 50, is a luxury campground, designed the way you'd design it if you had unlimited funds. There are 589 spaces, each one easy to back into, each one with full hookups and cable TV, access to a great golf course, a big club-house—everything, including a price tag of at least $29 per night. It's a really great place, so you might want to give it a try.

The second option is the **Jetty Park,** right on the ocean and the Banana River, within a hundred yards of where the cruise ships leave for Jamaica and within sight of the launching pads at **Cape Canaveral.** You can camp here for $5 per night. It's quiet (except when a launch is coming up), clean and well run. From either of these headquarters, you can visit the **Astronaut Hall of Fame,** (407) 269-6100; **Spaceport USA,** which is very much worth a visit; the **Kennedy Space Center; Cocoa** and **Cocoa Beach;** the **Merritt Island Wildlife Refuge;** or fish from charter boats—including ones that specialize in shark fishing!

Heading farther up the Atlantic Coast, our next stop is at **Marineland.** Leave northbound Interstate 95 on the state road that leads to **Flagler** and head north on the coast road to Marineland. Be sure to ask for your senior citizen discount when buying your tickets. The ticket office and movie theater are on the west side of the highway, where there's a large parking area. Take in the 3D movie at the theater first; it's a real treat. Then visit the few exhibits on the west side of the highway before heading over to the east side, where the best exhibits are located. Huge aquariums give you good views of more than one hundred species of ocean fish—including giant tarpon, big sharks and colorful reef fishes. The loudspeaker system will announce the dolphin show on the upper deck—the dolphins obviously enjoy playing games, and they shoot baskets, pass footballs and play catch with their trainer. They also perform tandem jumps through hoops and leap higher out of the water than you'd ever believe possible. It's a great show.

Performing dolphins, always crowd pleasers, leap through hoops at Florida's Marineland.

Next stop is historic **St. Augustine,** perhaps the oldest city in the United States. We chose a **KOA campground** there because it offered easy access to the ancient Spanish fort—the **Castillo de San Marcos**—and to the historic "old town" with its houses and stores dating back to the early 1600s. Another good campground close to St. Augustine's attractions is the **North Beach Camp Resort** located on the north beach at 4125 Coastal Highway, St. Augustine, FL 32084, (904) 824-1806 or 1-800-542-8316. Your Golden Age Passport gives you free entry to the walled fort of San Marcos, where you can walk its battlements, touch its cannons and learn about its fabulous history during the days when the English and Spanish fought each other for possession of the New World. Half a

mile south of the Castillo, you can visit reproductions of those tiny ships that brought the Spanish to Florida. There is much to see and do in this most ancient of all U.S. cities, established in 1565 by Don Pedro Menendez de Aviles. For 235 years, St. Augustine functioned as the capital of the Spanish Province of Florida.

As we left St. Augustine and headed for home, we stumbled upon one final Florida gem. About 5 miles east of **Green Cove Springs** on Highway 16 we decided to stop for the night at **Pacetti's Fish Camp,** simply because we were tired of driving that day. Our choice proved to be a good one, as we found good hookups and lots of shade in a rather haphazardly planned campground. The real gem, however, was the restaurant on the grounds. Situated right on Trout Creek, which leads into the St. John's River, this small restaurant really knows how to cook seafood, and we had one of the best meals of the entire trip—with excellent service and low prices. We've put that little out-of-the-way place on our list of places to go back to on our next Florida run. The phone number at the RV campground office is (904) 284-5356.

After a good night's sleep, we drove north to Interstate 10 to start the long run home, well satisfied with our Florida Sampler.

I know I've omitted hundreds of worthwhile stops, and I know that you probably know a score of attractions that we should have included, but remember that this is only a sampler, a beginning step toward enjoying one of our most interesting states—a state fortunate enough to avoid cold weather most of the year, making it a very attractive winter destination.

We suggest that you write to the Florida Department of Commerce, Division of Tourism, Collins Building, 107 Gaines Street, Tallahassee, FL 32399-2000, and ask for the *Vacation Guide Planner*. It will provide you with so many ideas that you'll have to spend the next two years in the Sunshine State.

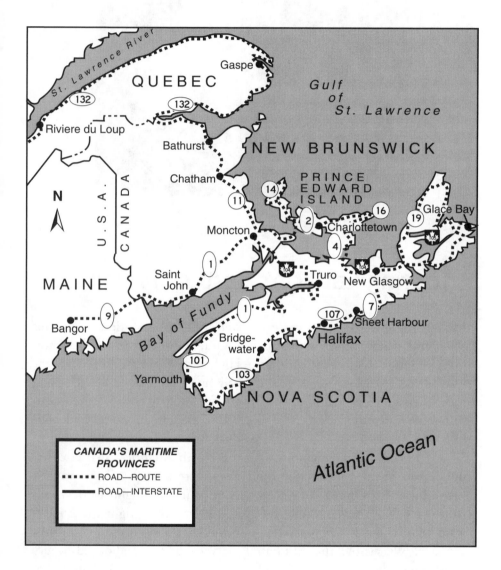

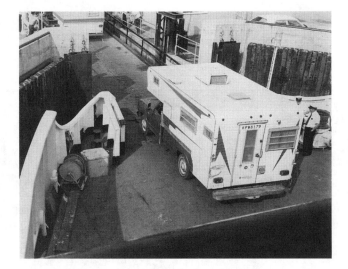

11
Touring Canada's Eastern Provinces

Maine is our most northeastern state. But when you go northeast from Maine, you enter the Canadian Maritime Provinces, some of the most rugged, most beautiful, most historically interesting territory in all of North America.

We have wonderful memories of our travels in the Maritimes—the Canadian Provinces of New Brunswick, Nova Scotia, Prince Edward Island and—*la belle province*—Quebec. We visited the Acadian lands, where the forced expulsion of the French colonists by the British was the basis of the Evangeline story. We saw Scottish games, including the throwing of the *caber*, ate lob-

ster at the lowest prices we've ever found, rounded the Cape Breton Highlands where the excellent highway hugs the rocky cliffs affording an unmatched view of the ocean below, bought mackerel and haddock direct from the cold waters of the North Atlantic—so fresh that they were still flipping—toured Louisbourg, the mighty fortress built by the French to fight the English before the expulsion of the Acadians, marveled at the landlocked beauty of *le Bras d'Or*, the golden arm of the Atlantic that penetrates deep into the easternmost part of Nova Scotia, ferried across to tiny Prince Edward Island, ate delicious oysters, dug clams on wide beaches, visited the city where *Anne of Green Gables* was written, enjoyed some of the best provincial campgrounds in all of Canada—but I'm getting ahead of my story. Let's take a tour together ...

On the first day of our journey, we crossed into Canada at **Calais,** traveled leisurely along the excellent Highway 1 to **St. Stephens by the Sea,** where we enjoyed our lunch, then on to **St. John,** with its famous "reversing falls" caused by the tremendously high tides in the Bay of Fundy, then on to **Moncton** to see famed **Magnetic Hill,** which presents an interesting optical illusion in which a golf ball seems to roll uphill—you really do have to see it to believe it. We found a campground for the night, boiled up a lobster dinner and savored our first day in the Maritimes. We studied the highway map, realizing that we had just crossed a narrow belt of New Brunswick's southern end. We decided to cross over into Nova Scotia (but don't worry, we'll be coming back to New Brunswick). But before we left, we toured **Fundy National Park** and visited the **Hopewell Rocks,** an interesting example of sculptured rocks carved by the ocean currents and tides.

Then it was back north to Moncton again and onto Highway 2 to enter Nova Scotia at **Amherst,** where we were met by a bonnie lass

playing the bagpipes. We toured an excellent **visitors' center** that provides a wonderful chance to plan your own trip through New Scotland. The visitors' center divides the scenic province into several different tours, and we wanted to see them all. We followed the main highway to **Truro,** then headed west on the south side of **Cobequid Bay** and the **Minas Basin,** driving through prosperous, well-kept countryside. Our destination was **Grande Pre National Historic Park,** which leads us directly into the story of the Acadians.

The French settled this southwestern half of the land we now call Nova Scotia and built a prosperous farming community that stretched along the sea-girt coast all the way to Yarmouth. These people were loyal French and devout Roman Catholics. When the fortunes of war turned their lovely homeland over to the British, they were faced with a real dilemma. They were asked to swear allegiance to the British crown—and remember, the King of England was the nominal head of the Anglican church. In other words, they were supposed to renounce both their loyalty to France and their religious beliefs. The great majority of them refused to do either, thus they were forcibly torn from the farms they had developed and exiled from Nova Scotia. The British sometimes separated mother and child, and husband and wife in this forced exodus. Some families were never reunited. Walking in the ornamental gardens of Grande Pre, we read again the story of Evangeline, in the place where it happened, and it had far more meaning for us this time.

The exiled Acadians sailed down our Atlantic Coast, searching for a hospitable place to settle. They were denied their request for land in Maryland, so they sailed around Florida and finally settled in the bayous of Louisiana. There the name Acadian got corrupted into "Cajun,"

Because storms are common on the seas around the Maritime Provinces, lighthouses are important aids to navigation.

and they remain a colorful element of Louisiana culture.

We found good campgrounds in **Margaretville** and in **Annapolis Royal,** where we toured **Port Royal National Park,** a bit of living history that re-creates the days of the French colonists. We found ourselves in **Yarmouth** on the third night and stayed in a good trailer park there. We were there at blueberry season and saw a café advertisement for "blueberry grunt." Being an explorer by nature, I ordered it and found that it was a huge piece of blueberry upside-down cake with whipped cream and half a pound of luscious berries.

Then it was on through **Lunenburg.** We drove **Lighthouse Drive** before picking a trailer park for the night, and the next day we visited one of the most beautiful spots in North America, the lighthouse at **Peggy's Cove.** Early morning fog covered the smooth rocks near the lighthouse and when sunlight was diffused through that fog, the result was surreal. We had to buy more film that day and overnighted in **Glen Margaret.**

Next stop **Halifax,** probably the most famous harbor in eastern Canada. We toured the "historic properties" area and restocked our kitchen cupboards at fine modern stores before taking off on the 180-mile drive through dozens of seacoast villages all the way to **Antigonish** (pronounced without any accent or stress, simply "ant-tig-awn-ish"). We camped for the night at **Whiddens Park,** in Antigonish. The French influence slowly fades into Scottish-English as you drive the south coast of Nova Scotia—restaurant cuisine also changes, from the delicious French to the "passable" Scottish to the not-so-hot English.

Leaving Antigonish, we crossed the narrow **Canso Causeway** and entered what I consider to be the most beautiful part of eastern Canada. Now is a good time to start looking for lobster bargains. Because opening and closing dates of lobster season vary widely throughout the Canadian Maritimes, it is wise to keep yourselves informed and dine where they're cheapest.

Our route ran along the **Bras d'Or,** the "golden arm" of the Atlantic that extends far inland, on through **Sydney,** where the coal mines extend far out beneath the sea floor, then south to **Fort Louisbourg.**

Next day was spent touring the historic fortress of Louisbourg, which is a fine example of "living history." Guards in French uniforms barred our entry to the colossal fortress and questioned us to determine that we were not "British loyalists" before they would let us in. The sprawling fortress contains shops and dining rooms, arsenals and troop barracks of the period, all restored with exacting care and staffed by men and women in French colonial costumes, complete down to the women gossiping out the back window. The great guns were never fired in battle, however, for the invading British simply attacked from a different direction. You should definitely take a whole day to tour this fortress, for it is one of the best examples of historic restoration north of Jamestown, Virginia. Tired from our day-long exploration, we continued on to **Seal Island** where we found a fine campground.

The next day was one of the high spots of the trip as we circled the **Cape Breton Highlands,** offering endless vistas of seascapes and low, rocky mountains. Tiny settlements hug the coast and supply homes for rugged lobster boats. At the northern end of the Highlands lies the tiny harbor and picturesque village of **Baie St. Lawrence,** and there we bought fresh fish for ridiculously low prices and feasted on the freshest seafood I've ever eaten. Some of the fish were still flipping when we bought them. I took a lot of pictures here of the photogenic boats rimming the harbor and the lovely white church in the center. We spent the night at **Dunvegan** on the western coast of the Highlands.

A word of warning might be in order. The road circling the Highlands is perfectly safe and easy to drive with no steep grades to climb and few sharp turns. But at times it rises above a sheer drop to the ocean below. If this bothers you, you might want to circle the Highlands in a clockwise direction, which would put your RV closer to the cliff side and away from the ocean side.

On the northwestern part of the circle drive, we saw the French tri-color flying in the breeze over lovely little seaside villages, defiant proof that not all of the French left when the Acadians were expelled.

Next we backtracked over the **Canso Canal** and on to **Pictou**, on the north side of western Nova Scotia, where we took the ferry across to **Prince Edward Island**, often referred to as simply P.E.I. The clock slows down on this island, and no one seems to be in a hurry. Gaudily painted farmhouses splash purple, kelly green and even pink across the flat landscape. The island has been described as two wonderful beaches separated by potato fields. There are many excellent harbors here and the best provincial park campgrounds in all of Canada. We slowed down to adjust to their pace as we toured lovely **Charlottetown,** dug clams on the flats, feasted on fresh vegetables sold at the roadside stands and had all the oysters we wanted. We went out on half-day fishing trips to try our luck at

handlining cod and haddock from the cold waters with an accommodating skipper who filleted all the fish we caught while regaling us with stories about the early days on this captivating island. I especially liked the little town of **North Lake,** where the tuna boats go out to do battle with the half-ton giants known as "horse mackerel." If you decide to try your luck at catching one of the big tuna, check the financial arrangements very closely. In most cases, the catch belongs to the boat; all you get is plenty of fresh air and exercise. With fresh raw tuna selling to the Japanese for well over $1.50 per pound, this is an important matter. If you want to try tuna fishing, write to North Lake Charter Association, North Lake, Prince Edward Island, Canada, for full information and prices.

You should have a road map of the island by this time, and that will enable you to locate **Brudenell River Provincial Park,** my nominee for best park in all of Canada. It's a good place to try your luck at offshore fishing for cod and haddock, at low prices.

We also recommend **Cabot Beach Provincial Park** and suggest you try your luck on a "head boat" out of **Malpeque.** The dollar value of the fish you bring back will more than pay for the fishing trip. While in Malpeque, be sure to visit the oyster farming research station at **Bideford** on the other side of the bay.

Unfortunately, you're not allowed to take samples.

P.E.I.'s provincial parks are the greatest attraction for RVers, and you should visit all of them. At **Lord Selkirk Provincial Park** we noticed people with shovels and pails following the receding tide as it uncovered the mudflats. One of the locals not only answered our questions about what was going on but actually provided us with the tools needed for clam digging. We found three kinds of clams—chowder clams, measuring less than 3 inches across, and the much larger bear paws and quahogs. We steamed them and ate our fill, then diced the rest into a chowder that was out of this world.

The time went by all too quickly on P.E.I., and we soon found ourselves in a campground at **Summerside,** awaiting the ferry trip back to the mainland in the morning. We didn't go back to Pictou but rather to **Cape Tormentine** in New Brunswick. We passed by campgrounds in **Chatham** and **Tracadie** before settling in one in **Dignard** for the night. The next day we toured a restored Acadian village at **Caraquet.** The French influence is very evident here in this point of land that juts out into the **Baie des Chaleurs.** The coastal villages are designed for visitors and their cameras—or so it seemed. Most of the people will speak to you in French, but if you

Canada's Maritimes make their living from the sea, as indicated by these commercial fishing boats.

answer in English they can usually handle that language also. It's fun to learn a bit of the beautiful French language. If you ask, *"Acceptez-vous cette carte de credit?"* the answer will surely be *"Oui!"* because they do accept your credit card. Pick up a little booklet put out by the tourism people that gives you a traveler's vocabulary. Be sure to use the phonetic pronunciation given in the book because French words are definitely not pronounced the way they are written.

West of **Bathurst, New Brunswick,** and close to **Dalhousie,** we crossed over into **Quebec** and found a nice campground in **Maria** for the night.

The next day we drove lazily along the seacoast to **Gaspé,** the town tipping the peninsula of the same name, and photographed famed **Percé Rock,** standing like a huge sentinel in the waters of the

Atlantic. We stayed the night at **Parc Caron,** where the proprietor didn't speak English at all. But, in one of those freak happenings that enliven travel in a foreign country, he and I both spoke Spanish. We got along famously. From Gaspé we took a boat ride out to **Ile Bonaventure,** a famous seabird rookery.

Leaving Gaspé we got a hint of what weather *can be* on this northern peninsula—we encountered heavy fog all the way to **Ste.-Anne-des-Monts,** and heavy rain the rest of the way to **Bic.** There we checked in and lit our RV furnace, although it was still August. The weather was cold that day, but our French-speaking hosts surely made us feel welcome in their campground.

The next day took us to **Quebec City,** which ranks as one of the most picturesque cities in the world. It also has some of the finest restaurants in the world and we tried three of them during our three-day stay in the ancient city. Be sure to eat at the **Chateau Frontenac** and the **House of the Ancient Canadians.** There was also a tiny place that called itself, in French, the "king's treat." Everything we ate in Quebec City *was* fit for a king. I have never eaten better, not even in Paris! We rode horse-drawn carriages through the walled old city, shopped in modern supermarkets and topped it all off by spending our nights in a KOA.

Then we rolled west on the super highway to **Montréal,** the second largest "French" city in the world, second only to Paris. I got a big surprise when studying the road map here, for I located the **Ile du Cadieux,** in **Two Mountain Lake** ("Lac des Deux Montagnes"). We visited the **Island of Cadieux** and left on Cadieux Boulevard, which deadended on Harwood Street—a really big coincidence, since my name is Cadieux and I live on Harwood in far-off Albuquerque! Plan to spend at least five days in cosmopolitan Montréal, taking time to visit its many different ethnic neighborhoods, tour its historic sites and above all, eat your fill of wonderful French cuisine. Just thinking about it whets my appetite and makes me want to return once more.

It's possible to make a similar trip through Canada's Maritimes with an organized caravan. You'll find no insurmountable handicaps if you travel alone, but the caravan will show you things you'd otherwise miss and—let's face it—caravans are fun! The following is a day-by-day account of a caravan we knew about a few years ago. A similar tour is offered by Tracks to Adventure, 1-800-351-6053. The price of their Viking tour is $4,125 for two people for 31 days. The cost includes 12 meals and 57 tours and events.

Itinerary

Day 1: Rendezvous in **Bar Harbor, Maine,** briefing by wagonmaster. Taken by bus on tour of Acadia National Park; back to camp for the evening to enjoy a New England clambake.

Day 2: Cross border into Canada, campground in **St. Andrews by the Sea.**

Days 3 and 4:

Lovely drive to campground at **Penobsquis, New Brunswick.** On the way tour **Fundy Park** and see the **Reversing Falls.**

Day 5: Travel to **Shubenacadie, Nova Scotia,** visiting **Springhill Coal Mines** and **Magnetic Hill** on the way.

Days 6 and 7:

In **Annapolis Royal,** with bus tour on the second day, including lunch prepared by local people. You also see **Fort Royal,** built in 1635, the oldest in all of Canada.

Day 8: Drive to **Yarmouth, Nova Scotia,** visit the **Fire Fighters Museum** and enjoy dinner courtesy of the wagonmaster.

Days 9, 10 and 11:

At **Indian Harbor, Halifax.** Enjoy a boat cruise around this famous harbor, the second largest in the world! Also a sightseeing tour of the city, along with a "historic" feast. Dinner provided at historic **Peggy's Cove.**

Day 12: Drive to **Antigonish,** arriving early enough to allow sightseeing and shopping in this pleasant city. Campground is only three blocks from main business district.

Day 13: Park at **Cape Breton** for a tour through the famous **Fort Louisbourg,** which we talked about earlier. Lunch included at the fort.

Days 14 and 15:

At **Bras d'Or, Nova Scotia.** Tour the famed **Cabot Trail.**

Day 16: Load your rig on the ferry bound for **Newfoundland!** Lots of time to enjoy wild and wonderful Newfoundland.

Days 17 and 18:

At **Rocky Harbor,** the only freshwater fjord in all of North America. Plan to take the **Viking Trail** to **St. Anthony.**

Day 19: Back to **Pasadena, Newfoundland,** for overnight stop.

Day 20: Ferry back to Nova Scotia and drive to **Caribou** where you'll board another ferry to **Prince Edward Island.**

Day 21:   Ferry over to P.E.I.

Days 22 and 23:

> At **North Murray Harbor, P.E.I.** Tour of the countryside, and lots of time to rest up, go fishing for the big ones, or whatever suits your fancy. The clock is much slower on this island, so relax.

Days 24, 25 and 26:

> At **Cornwall, P.E.I.** Attend a theater production of *Anne of Green Gables.* Lots of time for shopping and sightseeing.

Day 27:   You'll ferry back to New Brunswick and drive through much of its French section. Overnight at **Loggieville, New Brunswick.**

Day 28:   Tour a restored historic French village and overnight at **Bathurst, New Brunswick.**

Days 29 and 30:

> Drive the scenic coast of the north side of the **Bay des Chaleurs** and camp at **Percé,** where you'll be taken on a boat tour to famed bird aviary, **Ile Bonaventure.** Also a dinner at a very special place that you'll long remember.

Day 31:   Spend all day on a leisurely drive around the eastern end of the Gaspé Peninsula, with its spectacular coastal scenery. Overnight at **Ste.-Anne-des-Monts, Quebec.**

Day 32:   Overnight at Ste. Anne, Quebec, where the wagonmaster hosts a special "movie night."

Days 33, 34 and 35:

> Traveling days within Quebec with special stops to see the wood carvings along the highway, then a special grand tour of **Quebec City.** Lunch included at the **Chateau Frontenac.** Then a last farewell dinner together and we leave Quebec, headed for home.

If you can find a tour that ends in Quebec City, I would recommend it. You can spend more time in that lovely old city or continue on upriver (the St. Lawrence) to Montréal where you can spend months. Either way, as they say in French, *Laissez les bons temps roulez!,* which means "Let the good times roll!"

12

Vancouver Island: Canada's Pacific Playground

At more than 12,000 square miles, Vancouver Island isn't the largest Canadian island—some of its islands are much bigger. But no island on the face of the earth can offer more beauty, more lakes and rivers, lush rain forests, rugged rocky shorelines, longer sand beaches or more good campgrounds—more of everything that lures the RV traveler to visit.

The fact that you have to cross an arm of the ocean to reach the island isn't even a drawback; it's an insulating protection that slows the pace of homogenization among cities and provinces. Vancouver Island

is definitely not the same as the rest of British Columbia. It has a personality all its own and moves at a slower pace than most of Canada. Its people are more willing to smile at a stranger, more patient in answering questions, more willing to lend a helping hand. Above all, they are proud of their island—with good reason.

No matter which direction you come from, you have to take the ferry across to Vancouver Island. One ferry route leaves **Port Angeles,** in the state of Washington, and docks at the very lovely, very British capital of British Columbia. A second possibility is to arrive at **Port Hardy**, on the north end of the big island, by taking a ferry down from **Prince Rupert, B.C.**, or one of the B.C. ferries heading south from Alaskan waters. But the majority of RVs enter Vancouver Island by ferrying from **Tsawwassen** (near Vancouver city) to **Nanaimo** or **Swartz Bay** on the eastern side of the island.

British Columbia ferries are amazingly efficient as they carry thousands of vehicles per day on their regularly scheduled routes.

Let's begin our trip by crossing into Canada on Interstate 5 out of Washington. Customs inspection is usually cursory and quick, although I must have looked guilty on my last trip across. Canadian Customs and Immigration officials asked us to step out of our vehicle while they conducted a real search. I mean a *real* search. They went into every drawer and cupboard on my ancient Southwind, removed and replaced every single item in my refrigerator and freezer compartment, even checked the pockets of clothing hanging in the closets. There was nothing to find, so I wasn't worried, but it did delay us half an hour. Canadian rules prohibit almost all firearms, so don't try to sneak a gun through. Be honest in answering questions about the amount of al-coholic beverages you carry. In fact, if you obey the rules, you have nothing to worry about—and the time loss will be very small.

After clearing customs, you'll notice that U.S. Interstate 5 has become Canada's Highway 99. Follow 99 to exit 28, where you'll turn south on 17. This road leads directly to the **Tsawwassen-Nanaimo** and **Tsawwassen-Swartz Bay** ferries, and if it fits your schedule, you can drive directly onto the ferry. If you want to rest up and ferry across in the morning, you would do well to stay at **Parcanada** at the intersection of 52nd Street and Highway 17. Watch for a small sign telling you where to turn off. The camp is on your right. The park is well laid out, clean and well run with lots of hot water in the showers. The campground map shows 126 campsites with another 31 for tents only. This park features a gift shop, convenience store, swimming pool, game room and lounge.

When you're rested up, you'll find that the ferry terminal is only about 5 miles farther down the road on 17. There a well-planned system of lane markers will guide you to the pay booth, where you'll be asked your total vehicle length and given a ticket, along with written instructions as to which lane to go to for boarding purposes. Our 31-footer's fare was $67 in Canadian funds each way—which is cheap for entry into wonderful Vancouver Island. You'll be told to turn off all propane, and given a red sticker to place over the valve to show that it is off (I don't know why, however, since no one ever looks to see if you've complied with regulations). Expertly efficient employees guide you on board and to your place on the lower deck of the huge ferry, the *Queen of Alberni.* The entire loading operation—putting literally hundreds of vehicles aboard—takes less than 15 minutes.

You lock your rig and ride two escalators to the upper decks where there's a good cafeteria and a lunch counter. If you plan to eat breakfast on board, go immediately to the cafeteria to avoid the rush. Comfortable armchair lounges are located fore and aft, but you'll probably want to travel out on deck so you can enjoy the magnificent scenery.

Unloading takes less time than loading so when the all-too-short trip (an hour and a half to Swartz Bay, two hours to Nanaimo) is over, you are on the road quickly and smoothly. I always ferry to Nanaimo, because I want to head to my favorite spots first. On the right side of Highway 19 heading north you'll find several excellent grocery stores. I recommend the giant supermarkets named Overwaitea, pronounced *Over-wait-tee.* They're found in all principal towns on the island.

Our first destination is the pro-vincial park called **Miracle Beach,** with 191 lovely shaded campsites— no hookups, but a dump station and hot showers in a clean building. And free firewood! As soon as we got situated, I headed for the beach, only a hundred yards away, and sat atop big logs washed ashore by the wind and waves, and gazed across the salty miles to the distant mainland of British Columbia, where snow still capped the mountains. The sea was so calm that the image of the distant mountains was mirrored on its smooth surface. Great white clouds floated high in a brilliant blue sky. The only sounds were those of children at play in the trailer park behind me and the far-off rhythmic thrumming of a diesel tug pulling a long string of barges far across the water. Peace and quiet washed over me and the tensions of the many miles slowly faded away.

Plan to spend several days here in the peaceful serenity of Miracle Beach. Beachcombing is good and the ebb and flow of the tides is interesting enough for further study.

The price tag for the Miracle Beach Campground is $14.50 Canadian (from here on, I'll not bother to write "Canadian" because you'll take that for granted). When I last traded U.S. dollars for Canadian, the exchange rate gave me $245 Canadian for $200 American. But this changes regularly so check the exchange rate on the financial pages of your local newspaper or ask at the nearest bank. If you change money at a Canadian bank, you'll be assured of the correct rate. If you change money at stores or motels, you'll be given less Canadian for your U.S. dollar. Canadians seem to agree that prices in the states are great bargains, and many of them come to our country to buy groceries and clothing.

If you must have hookups, check with the **Miracle Beach Resort**; it has a limited number of campsites right on the water. The resort is reached by driving through the provincial park. Phone (250) 337-5171.

Our next destination is the town of **Campbell River**, "Tyee Capital of the World." A "tyee" is a king or chinook salmon weighing over 30 pounds. Anglers come from all over the world to try their luck at landing one of the huge fish. Guides are available and boats for rent are plentiful. The best deal for the beginner is to employ a guide with boat, which will cost about $45 per hour. We stayed at the **Campbell River Fishing Village and RV Park**, right on the beach, which was a very convenient location because guides and boats are available for rent at the RV Park. This camp is located at 260 South Island Highway, Campbell River, B.C., Canada V9W 1A4, (250) 287-3630. All sites have ocean views

and picnic tables and cost about $13 per night. It's best to call ahead when the tyee are in the straits, as Campbell River is mighty busy at that time.

Another recommended RV park is located halfway between **Courtenay** and Campbell River. **The Pacific Playgrounds** at **Saratoga Beach,** 9082 Clarkson Drive, Black Creek, B.C., Canada V9J 1B3, (250) 337-5600, offers 240 spacious sites, 140 of them with full hookups. If you're bringing a boat, there is a fine marina. If you've left the boat at home, charters and guides are available right on the site. Without a boat, cutthroat trout can be caught in the Oyster River from mid-August to late October.

We stayed here at the Campbell River, right on the Coastal Highway and within 100 feet of the ocean.

Boats launched at Telegraph Cove are within short distance from excellent Salmon Fishing.

Another RV park very worthy of mention is the **Salmon Point RV Park and Marine,** located at 2176 Salmon Point Road in Campbell River, (250) 923-6605. They have 150 full hookup RV sites, all marina and charter facilities and a heated swimming pool.

Campbell River is a full-service town, with good shopping for almost everything. It's also a good spot to buy prawns and salmon and other goodies from the sea—in restaurants or in bulk to cook in the comfort of your own rig.

Following Highway 19 north from Campbell River, you'll find that trailer parks become scarcer, and the scenery even more beautiful. Don't pass up the rest area at **Seymour Narrows.** It's in the right location for a coffee break, anyway. Here you can get a good look at the narrow, current-swept passage that once was a barrier to navigation because of "Ripple Rock," a submerged danger in midchannel. The obstruction was blasted away many years ago and that made the passage much safer, although it is still narrow and swift.

Highway 19 leads you north from Seymour Narrows to our next destination, **Telegraph Cove** (and you should start watching for the road turning off to the east from 19 after you pass the tiny town of Wass). You'll be traveling through unmatched forest scenery—and receiving an education in forest management. These forests are managed by the giant MacMillan-Bloedel Company and the Nimpkish Corporation. Both companies have erected small, unobtrusive signs informing you, for example, that "This forest was cut in 1921, reforested in 1923, thinned in 1938 and harvested again in 1992. It will be replanted in 1994." It seems to me that the cutting of our great forests is made more palatable in light of such evidence that sustainable yields can continue forever if forests are managed intelligently.

Turning off on the road to Telegraph Cove, you'll start watching for big trucks carrying the giant logs of the forestry industry. A quarter of a century ago, when we first visited Vancouver Island, these trucks acted as if they—and only they—had the right to travel these roads, and gave us some scary moments when we met on narrow roads. Today, things are much better and the logger trucks gave us every consideration. There's even an educational turnout at the big **Beaver Cove** log sorting facility, which is surely worth a stop.

Tiny Telegraph Cove offers a very small parking lot, but you have to find room because this is the office for the **Telegraph Cove Campground,** one of the most beautiful in all of Canada. Check with the people at the Boardwalk Café to arrange for your space in the campground, located about 2 miles farther along the winding road. If you find room to park, this would be a good time to stroll the historic boardwalk and read the plaques that explain the story of Telegraph Cove. At the same time, you might want to book fishing charters out of Telegraph Cove. Although the emphasis here—as in all of Vancouver Island—is on salmon, Telegraph Cove charters offer a short run in protected waters to some of the best halibut fishing to be found anywhere. For my money, fresh halibut is the tastiest fish that swims, far better than the (still tasty) frozen product. At Telegraph Cove, the schedules for catching the various species of salmon goes like this: chinook and coho, best from June 15 through September 15; pink and

sockeye salmon, best from July 10 to September 5; northern coho are best from August 15 through the end of September.

From mid-June into October, this is a good place to go on whale-watching trips when the mighty mammals can be found close to shore, in protected waters that reduce the risk of seasickness. The best known of the whale-watching trips is offered by **Stubbs Island Charters LTD,** addressed at P.O. Box 2-2, Telegraph Cove, B.C., Canada V0N 3J0, (250) 928-3185, or 1-800-665-3066 within British Columbia. They operate two 60-foot vessels, the *Lukwa* and *Gikumi,* offer senior rates and feature a short run to the whale-watching grounds, where you are almost certain to see the misnamed killer whales at close range.

The campground at Telegraph Cove offers full hookups at $18.50 per day for the privilege of camping under tall trees in a shaded valley within walking distance of the ocean and of the town (village?) of Telegraph Cove. Although there are 125 sites and the location is definitely off the beaten path, it's best to call ahead to find out if sites are available. This is especially true during the salmon fishing times, for this spot is well known to dedicated salmon anglers.

We hated to leave, but there is much more to see on Vancouver Island, so we headed back to Highway

19 and turned northward for the very short run to **Port McNeil,** where we bought groceries and gasoline, watched a pair of adult bald eagles snatch fish out of the mirror-smooth seas and visited with commercial fishermen on the docks. The water was so clear that we could see Dungeness crabs walking along the sand and rock bottom, and also multilegged starfish as big as dinner plates.

Port McNeil offers several good campsites, including **Broughton Strait Campground,** which claims to be only a ten-minute walk from the shopping center; **Marble River,** which offers 33 sites half-an-hour's drive from Port McNeil; **Cluxewe Campground,** with 30 sites, 15 miles north of Port McNeil; and **Alder Bay Campground,** 7 miles east of Port McNeil, offering full hookups right on the water. There are other campsites offered by the big timber companies and a visit to the **Port McNeil Infocentre** will give you up-to-date information on these.

If you love to get away from it all and see seldom-visited places, now is your chance, as there are regularly scheduled ferry trips to the town of **Scintula** (a settlement of Finlanders) on **Malcolm Island,** and to **Alert Bay.** The ferry is plenty big enough, carrying 27 vehicles and 293 people at one time. It's best to leave the big rig in one of Port McNeil's campgrounds and use your tow vehicle for these trips.

If you're still craving seafood, we'd like to recommend the **Dalewood Inn Restaurant**—hours of operation vary, so call ahead to make sure they're open; phone is (250) 956-3304.

We advise the more adventurous RVer to get a copy of the Port McNeil Forest map, which shows the locations of and roads to dozens of primitive campgrounds, most of them reached by logging roads. The same Infocentre can advise you as to which campgrounds are suited to your RV type. This map will also cover the territory around our next and most northern stop.

Port Hardy, the northern terminus of Coastal Highway 19, is also the point of embarkation for B.C. ferries heading up the Inland Passage and for travelers returning from Alaska. From Port Hardy, logging company roads and provincial roads lead to some of the most isolated attractions on our tour of this wonderful island—places like **Cape Scott Provincial Park** and **Raft Cove Provincial Marine Park.** These roads offer access to infrequently fished or visited lakes and rivers whose clear, cold waters just beg for exploration by anglers. Before setting out on your exploration, you *must* check with local forestry people to see if a particular road is open to RV travel and to ascertain its condition. If you're up to the challenges, you'll visit some of the most beautiful and rugged country in Canada. But look before you leap—roads on the forestry map are classified "gravel road, rough road and very rough road."

For current information about roads, lakes and campsites on the Port McNeil Forest District, call (250) 956-5000. Questions about provincial parks within British Columbia should be phoned to (250) 387-4550. Infocentre in Port Hardy can be contacted at (250) 949-7622, and the Infocentre at Port McNeil can be contacted at (250) 956-3131.

We did our exploring out of Port Hardy while headquartering at **Sunny Sanctuary Campground,** which is on Highway 19 and borders the Quatze River. When we were first there, my wife called out in surprise, "Chuck, look at the rabbit!" At first I thought it was a wild cottontail, but it was too dark in color. Then we saw another, almost pure black, and another that was gray and brown and white and almost every other color. They run loose all over the campground and kept us amused with their antics. They were totally unafraid of people. In addition, a large flock of Canada geese rested on the shoals in the Quatze River and flew overhead with mellifluous honking.

Sunny Sanctuary offers 70 very large, level sites with all hookups, showers and rest rooms, as well as a convenience store and storage facilities in case you want to leave your vehicle and travel north on the ferry without it. It made a fine location from which to explore this northernmost end of Vancouver Island.

It was time to head back south, and we retraced our route all the way to **Parksville** and the junction with Highway 4, headed for **Cathedral Grove, Port Alberni** and to the "life on the edge" towns of **Tofino** and **Ucluelet.**

Cathedral Grove is located just a few miles west of the junction.

At Cathedral Grove, trails lead you into the midst of giant Douglas firs.

There is parking space on both sides of this busy highway, but parking is often filled to the brim. Park carefully and be wary if you have to cross the highway. You are entering a wonderful place where six-hundred-year-old Douglas firs tower above you, where the sounds of automobile traffic are muted by the giant trees and where each footfall is cushioned by pine needles shed over the centuries. Most of the area is so shaded by the lofty giants that not enough sunlight reaches the forest floor to support green plants. Where the sun penetrates, there is a lush growth of ferns and devil's club. We found ourselves speaking quietly, as people do in church, and surely this is an outdoor cathedral. You feel very small indeed when walking among these forest giants.

Trails lead you through the grove, and explanatory signs help you understand what you are seeing. Some of the trees are much older, but the majority are the result of a fire about six hundred years ago. What does fire have to do with the birth of a forest? Read the explanatory signs and you'll learn.

Leaving Cathedral Grove, Highway 4 continues through forest scenery to the bustling city of **Port Alberni,** situated at the top of Alberni Inlet, which leads to Barkley Sound and out into the Pacific. Forestry and fishing have made Port Alberni prosperous, but in my mind Alberni is best known as the home port of the M.V. *Lady Rose.* Built in 1937 in Scotland, the *Lady Rose* has seen service on the run to Bamfield and the run to Ucluelet for more than half a century. It is the lifeline of communication for distant outposts along the waterway—their source of everything from milk and the daily newspaper to mining supplies and commercial fishing and logging gear. She's definitely a working vessel, but she'll take along one hundred passengers on her scenic day-long run. There's a café on board for your enjoyment.

The *Lady's* year-round schedule has Tuesday, Thursday and Saturday sailings to Bamfield and back. She leaves the Port Alberni dock promptly at 8:00 A.M. and returns at 5:30 P.M. In the summer, from June 2 through September 15, there are additional sailings to Ucluelet and Tofino and through the Broken Islands Group. You can get full information by writing to the Alberni Marine Transportation, P.O. Box 188, Port Alberni, B.C., Canada V9Y 7M7, (250) 723-8313. Incidentally, you'll find red leaflets about the *Lady Rose* in the pamphlet racks onboard the big ferry that brings you across from the mainland.

A newer and larger vessel, the M.V. *Frances Barkley,* has been added to the fleet and is now in service on some of these voyages. It is bigger and better but lacks the charm of the *Lady Rose.* Be sure you know which vessel you're buying tickets for. But with either vessel, a day-long cruise on the waters of Alberni Inlet and Barkley Sound is a pleasant change of pace, an opportunity to see bald eagles and seabirds, to watch for whales and to gain a glimpse into the unique life of the isolated places along the waterway.

There are many good campgrounds in and around to Port Alberni, and you can get current information as to vacancies by visiting the Tourist Information Center as you come into town from the east. We stayed at the **Somass Motel and RV Park,** which offers water, electric hookups and a sanitary station. This small campground is located at 5279 River Road, Port Alberni, B.C., Canada V9Y 6Z3, which is very convenient to downtown and to Port Alberni Marina at 5104 River Road, a good place to get full information about salmon charters. King salmon runs are expected June through October, and there's a big run of sockeye (red salmon) during the same months. For more information, call (250) 723-8022.

While in Alberni we made a day trip to **Sproat Lake,** where the huge flying boats, adapted for fire fighting, can be seen. These monsters scoop up tons of water from the lake

and fly to the forest fire, where they drop the water on the fire. We spent another day exploring downtown Port Alberni and especially **Harbour Quay,** which displays local arts and crafts in specialty shops. A couple of blocks from Harbour Quay, right next to the railroad line, is a good place to buy fresh seafood. We bought giant prawns and fresh halibut and had a feast in our own motor coach at day's end.

Now, before continuing west on Highway 4, check the brakes, brake fluid, coolant and transmission fluid to make sure that everything is in readiness for the trip to Tofino and Ucluelet. For the first part of the trip, you'll travel beside beautiful Sproat Lake on a good blacktop road. Leaving Sproat Lake, the road narrows and begins to twist and turn, to climb and descend, with abrupt hairpin turns, steep climbs that will heat up your radiator and long descents that'll heat up your brakes. The road isn't dangerous, but does require you to *drive* all the way and that your rig be in good shape. When you leave Sproat Lake's beauty behind, you have just a short run before the road skirts along **Kennedy Lake,** one of the most beautiful on the island. Viewpoints are few and far between, so keep your eye on the road and let your copilot describe it to you. You'll be coming back this way, and then it will be your turn to gaze while he or she does the driving.

Highway 4 comes to a "T" with Ucluelet to your left and Tofino to your right—each is worth a visit, so take your choice. Both towns have recently awakened to the value of tourism but are still dependent upon the salmon and logging industries. They have good harbors providing safe moorings away from the sometimes rambunctious Pacific. Either town can serve as a headquarter location for visiting the **Pacific Rim National Park.**

We selected the **Ucluelet Campground,** which overlooks the harbor and is within walking distance to the tiny town and its best restaurants. It has 85 sites, some with full hookups. The address is P.O. Box 777, Ucluelet, B.C., Canada V0R 3A0, (250) 726-4355. This campground is always sold out when the salmon are in, so be sure to call ahead. Reservations are taken only for stays of four or more days.

Another approved campground is the **Island West Fishing Resort,** P.O. Box 32, Ucluelet, B.C., Canada V0R 3A0, (250) 726-7515. This one has 34 spaces and, like the Ucluelet Campgound, is always full in salmon season.

For a unique dining experience we recommend the *Canadian Princess,* a ship converted into a restaurant and lounge. It's right in the in-ner harbor, just a few blocks from the Ucluelet Campground. In addition to prime rib and an early fisherman's breakfast buffet, they offer lots of seafood and an excellent salad bar. They also have ten 50-foot boats available for charters of all kinds. Telephone is (250) 726-7771.

For **salmon charters** out of Ucluelet, call the **Ucluelet Chamber of Commerce** at (250) 726-4641 for names and telephone numbers of approved skippers. This tiny village calls itself the "Whale-Watching Capital of the World" and stakes this claim on the annual migration of Pacific gray whales that pass close to town each spring on the northbound leg of their journey. About 19,000 of these giants travel from their calving and mating grounds on the west coast of the Baja Peninsula of Mexico, bound for feeding grounds in the Arctic. Some of the gray whales take up permanent residence near Ucluelet and Tofino and can be seen all summer long. For a real thrill, go out to visit the whales in a Zodiac, an inflatable rubber boat that is surprisingly strong and completely safe. This type of whale watching will put you in close proximity to the giants. The killer whale, common on the east coast of the island, is almost never seen in the colder waters of the Pacific on the west coast. Conversely, the bigger gray whales are rarely seen in the enclosed waters along the eastern coast of Vancouver Island.

Tofino serves the northern end of the Pacific Rim National Park, as Ucluelet serves the southern end. Recommended campgrounds in the Tofino area include **Crystal Cove Beach Resort,** which offers 65 sites about 2 miles south of Tofino, on or close to the beach, full and partial hookups, hot showers and rest rooms. Prices range from $25 to $35 depending upon the hookups provided. Their address is P.O. Box 559, Tofino, B.C., Canada V0R 2Z0, (250) 725-4213.

Sixteen sites with partial hookups are available at **Mackenzie Beach Resort,** about 1 mile south of Tofino. They boast an indoor pool, which you'll welcome after you've tried swimming in the cold Pacific. Their address is P.O. Box 12, Tofino, B.C., Canada V0R 2Z0, (250) 725-3439.

Another approved Tofino campground is the **Bella Pacifica Campground,** also located on Mackenzie Beach. Their address is simply Tofino, B.C., Canada V0R 2Z0, (250) 725-3400. They offer 176 sites ranging in price from $24 to $33 depending upon what hookups are provided.

A word of warning about **Pacific Rim Resort Campground,** 4 miles south of Tofino. Despite its name, it is not managed by the Pacific Rim National Park. It does not bear the seal of approval of the British Columbia Ministry of Tourism. On a recent trip, we heard nothing good about this campground, and we do not recommend it. We hope it will improve because it offers 120 sites with all hookups.

How about camping in Pacific Rim National Park?

Stop at the **information center** operated by the national park, located on Highway 4, right at the entrance to the **Long Beach Unit** of the Pacific Rim National Park. They will advise you as to the availability of campgrounds suitable for RVs. This Information Center is staffed from Easter through mid-October; their phone number is (250) 726-4212.

We camped at **Green Point,** at the southern end of **Long Beach,** and within hiking distance of **Wickaninnish Beach,** south of our campsite. These two expansive sand beaches offer wonderful beachcombing opportunities. We once saw a small four-wheel-drive vehicle out on the hard-packed sand. The driver got out for a lengthy photo session, leaving the motor running while he snapped many pictures of his lovely companion. But the vibration of the motor caused his wheels to sink slowly into the sand. He had difficulty driving out of his predicament, and if he hadn't had four-wheel drive, he'd never have made it.

Tofino slightly outdoes Ucluelet in providing charter fishing, whale-watching trips and general seaborne sightseeing. Get close to the whales in a 24-foot Zodiac, operated by **Remote Passages** in Tofino, (250) 725-3330. Whale-watching trips of three hours cost $50 for adults, and $35 for children under 12. They provide full wetsuits for warmth and safety. This is an adventure—live a little!

If you prefer whale watching on a larger boat, **Jamie's Whaling Station,** (250) 725-3919, offers the 65-foot *Lady Selkirk*. Whale-watching trips cost $70 for adults and $65 for seniors on the larger boats. They also offer Zodiac trips ($50 for adults and seniors), scheduled daily in the summer, as well as whale-watching and wildlife-viewing trips that end with a swim in the hot springs. Delightful!

After you've had your fill of walking the long sandy beaches, eyeballing whales at close range, fishing for salmon and halibut and swimming in the hot springs, it's time to retrace your path through that magnificent scenery back through Port Alberni to Parksville and head south.

Campgrounds and trailer parks are found everywhere from Parksville through Nanaimo and Duncan on down to Victoria, the capital of British Columbia and one of the loveliest cities to be found anywhere. En route, be sure to stop at the **Indian Cultural Center** in **Duncan,** one of the very best places to purchase authentic Cowichan sweaters. Made by the Cowichan tribe of Indians, they are not for sale in the town of Cowichan but are sold only by the Indian Cultural Center in Duncan. The sweaters are loosely woven heavy wool in natural colors—if they want brown or black, they use wool from a sheep of that color. They are definitely not cheap—in 1993 we paid $239 for an extra large sweater—but they are incredibly warm and last forever. Sweaters we bought twenty-five years ago are still doing duty in the winter months.

Victoria is one of the most interesting and beautiful cities in the world of RVing. We camped at the **West Bay Marina and RV Park,** right on the harbor but across the bay from the tall buildings of the inner harbor and the seat of government. We parked the rig for four days and used the tiny harbor ferry boats to get around. It costs $3 per ride, but that was a good deal compared to unhooking the rig and trying to find a parking place downtown.

To locate this wonderful trailer park, just take Government Street north from downtown to Pandora

Street. Take a left on Pandora and cross the bridge. You'll find yourself on Esquimalt, which you follow to Head Street. Turn left again on Head Street, which leads directly to the well-marked trailer park. The address is 453 Head Street, Victoria, B.C., Canada V9A 5S1, (250) 385-1831. Calling ahead is a good idea as this park is very popular and usually filled in July and August—even some days in June.

We drew space 12 where we could loll away the evening hours in our lawn chairs as we watched the sunset and the lights coming on across the bay. (I hate to rave about any trailer park, but this one is exceptionally good.)

Our first evening there, we felt like walking to get the kinks out of travel-wearied legs, so we strolled the picturesque boardwalk along the shore from the head of the **Marina Spinakers Restaurant**. Be warned, it is several miles, but we oldsters made it easily and so can you. If you go early, you won't have to wait for a table. If you plan on eating after 6:00 P.M., it's best to phone ahead for a reservation. The food is delicious, featuring seafood but also offering many beef, veal and pork dishes. Spinakers brews its own beer and ale and offers a choice of seven locally brewed suds—we tried Weizenbrau and Dunkelweizen, and plan on trying Doc Hadfield's Pale,

Promenading along the Inner Harbour of Victoria's waterfront, we saw jugglers, musical acts, ferries coming from and going to the United States and much more.

Mitchells CSB, Scottish Amber Ale, Mt. Tolmie Dark and Oatmeal Stout on future visits.

There is so much to see and do that your days will fly by all too quickly. Pickups can be arranged for tours to **Butchart Gardens**, one of the world's foremost floral displays. Visit the oldest **Chinatown** in Canada, especially the famous **Gate of Harmonious Interest,** and walk through **Fan Tan Alley.** Tour the **Government Street shopping district,** take a guided tour through the **House of Parliament,** visit the **Royal British Columbia Museum** with its wonderful exhibits on the Native people who lived here long before Captain George Vancouver sailed these waters. Visit the venerable **Victoria Hotel** with its air of colonial grandeur. If you want to be really "in," savor high tea at the Victoria Hotel—live it up just this once! At the corner of Wharf and Government Streets, you'll find the **Infocentre,** whose knowledgeable and friendly staff will answer all of your questions and assist you with tickets to everything. A few blocks away is the **Undersea Gardens,** well worth a visit. If you get tired of walking, take a double-decker bus tour to see the sights. If even the double-deckers are too fast for you, you can tour by horse-drawn carriages.

If you can't schedule yourself into the West Bay Marina and RV Park, don't despair—there are many excellent trailer parks in and around Victoria.

Fort Victoria RV Park, located at 340 Island Highway 1A in Victoria, offers 300 full hookups and is served by city bus lines, making trips to the attractions less expensive. For reservations call (250)

You can explore Victoria the easy way, via horse-drawn carriage.

479-8112, or fax them at (250) 479-5806.

If you're addicted to KOA campgrounds, there are two good ones here. **Victoria West KOA,** located 16 miles north of Victoria, near the Butchart Gardens, offers peace and quiet away from the city bustle. Their mailing address is P.O. Box 103, Malahat, B.C., Canada V0R 2L0, phone and fax (250) 478-3332. The **Victoria East KOA,** mailing address RR 1, 3000 KOA Road, Saanichton, B.C., Canada V0S 1M0, is located 10 miles north of the inner harbor on Highway 17. Incidentally, this park is located near the Waddingly Dog Inn. I never visited that establishment but the name is certainly intriguing.

One more campground worthy of mention is the **Thetis Lake Campground,** ten minutes from the city center, offering 100 sites with full hookups and all the amenities. It is located at 1938 TransCanada Highway 1, RR 6, Victoria, B.C., Canada V9B 5T9, (250) 478-3845. The view is spectacular and the location is great for exploring the vicinity.

For help in exploring the city, get a copy of the B.C. Transit *Rider's Guide* from the Infocentre at Government and Wharf Streets. You'll be surprised at how many attractions you can visit by bus, thus avoiding the problem of parking a large rig.

While at the Infocentre, pick up a copy of the *Visitor's Guide to Victoria and Vancouver Island*, which will lead you to many new attractions and regret the ones you've missed for lack of time.

We hope you'll plan sufficient time to really get to know this fascinating city. How about a game of cricket? Or lawn bowling? Have you seen the hanging baskets of flowers that are one of the trademarks of this most British city in Canada? Were the rhododendrons in bloom when you visited? If not, you'll surely want to plan another visit.

When your visit to Victoria and Vancouver Island comes to an end, you still have an enjoyable sea voyage ahead of you. Two top choices are ferries from Nanaimo to Port Angeles, Washington, and from Swartz Bay to Tsawwassen, B.C. If you're headed farther east in the States, by all means take the Swartz Bay to Tsawwassen ferry. It's cheaper than the one to Port Angeles, sails more frequently and makes a faster crossing. Looking back at the scenic islands guarding the approaches to Swartz Bay, I always get a lump in my throat when I realize that I'm actually leaving one of the most fascinating places for an RVer, beautiful Vancouver Island. But then someone points out a whale cavorting in the clear waters and the melancholy vanishes—who could feel sad after having seen one of the greatest destinations for every RVer?

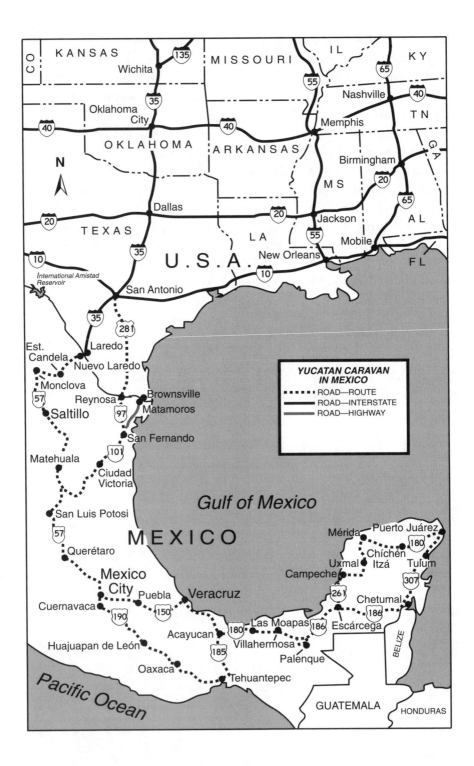

13
Mexico's Yucatan Peninsula: Land of the Maya

I would call this tour of the Land of the Maya *the* greatest of all RV trips, but that would show my prejudice— I was one of the four people who first scouted out a caravan route to this remote corner of Mexico. With the man who first popularized Mexican caravans, the legendary Gil Andrews, and longtime wagonmasters Bill Wallace and Will Hardy, we drove from El Paso to Tampico and Tuxpan on the Gulf of Mexico, then followed the delightful coastal route through Veracruz and Coatzacoalcos and entered Maya land at the breathtakingly beautiful ruins of Palenque.

Completely enthralled by the architectural grandeur of the Mayan ruins, we continued on to visit Uxmal, Edzna, Kabah, Coba, Tulum, Chichén Itzá and many lesser-known archaeological sites. We camped at night on lovely white sand beaches at Campeche, Laguna de Terminos, Cancún, Tulum and many other spots that begged us to stay. We found very few good trailer parks, but there were a few—Graham Brothers' Ranch near Coatzacoalcos, one at Piste near Chichén Itzá, a lovely spot without hookups on the beach north of Cancún where the ferry takes off for Isla Mujeres.

We were enthralled by the beauty of this area, and I was captivated by the mysteries of the Maya—I still am, thirty years later. I've since made nine trips to the Yucatán as a leader of caravans and a couple trips on my own, just to satisfy my curiosity. Each trip gave me a few answers to the mystery of the Maya, and brought up ten more questions.

What mystery? Without the wheel, the ancient Maya built smooth rock-paved roads leading for hundreds of miles across the jungle to link great cities. Without optical glass or timepieces of any kind, they aligned their buildings with the vernal equinox of Venus and with the autumnal risings of the Pleiades (the stars we sometimes call the Seven Sisters). They learned to predict eclipses of the sun and moon, and used astronomy to determine the best planting dates for their crops. The ruling caste also used their knowledge of astronomy to hold the respect and veneration—perhaps even the fear—of the common people.

Fascinated by the concept of time, the Maya recorded the dates of important events: the assumption of power by a new leader, the conquest of a neighboring people, the marriage of one of their god-rulers, the birth of an heir apparent. These dates were meticulously carved into the sides of huge pillars of stone, known as stelae. Their social structure was amazingly complicated, and their passion for building and rebuilding great temples to their gods continues to amaze us even today.

We know that the Maya populated what is now Guatemala and much of the Yucatán Peninsula before the time of Christ, but the peak of their civilization was from about A.D. 900 to A.D. 1100. Then, about two hundred years before the Spanish conquistadores arrived, the great civilization disappeared, and no one knows why. There is no evidence of a natural catastrophe such as an earthquake or a great flood; there is no evidence of warfare contributing to their demise. But the great civilization of the Maya was gone, its main temple cities depopulated, long before the arrival of the Europeans, who conquered all of Mexico and all of Mesoamerica.

Estimates of the total population of the Mayob (the Mayan name for their land) range as high as 6 million, and it could have been much higher. Some who believe in fantasy think that the Mayans just sailed away across the sea! How could you move millions of people in the sailing ships of that era? Besides, look at the faces of today's Mayans—and find their counterparts in the fabulous sculptures of the ancient Maya. Their civilization may have disappeared, the Mayans themselves didn't go anywhere. Some of their tribes (such as the Lacandon) still live as the ancients did, but without the leadership that built Copán and Tikal and Palenque—without the artistic ability that built the towering Castillo at Uxmal.

Much of the written literature of the Maya was deliberately destroyed by Bishop Diego de Landa because he thought it to be the writing of the devil. This same de Landa later became the greatest student of the Maya and must be credited with much of what we know about the Maya. Students and scientists from all over the world have explored the mysteries of the Maya, discovering how they counted and deciphering most of the hieroglyphics carved into the limestone of their jungle-shrouded cities. The spoken language of the Maya remains intact, and the Yucatecas have resisted the inroads of Spanish culture far more successfully than any other Native civilization in all of multitribal Mexico.

If you have time to visit only one site, by all means visit **Palenque.** The best way to make your first trip to Mayaland is with an organized caravan of RV travelers. If you do this, you'll overcome the handicap of not knowing the language because every caravan worth its salt enlists the services of native-speaking Mexicanos.

It also has the great advantage of having your overnight parking campgrounds already selected and (in most cases) prepaid. The wagonmaster and tailgunner are experienced enough to make sure that you don't drive right by the off-road attractions, and the fact that a mechanic is following along behind you takes much of the worry out of Mexican travel. And then, too, the social life of a caravan adds much to your enjoyment of the trip.

When I was leading caravans to the land of the Maya, we took forty-five days to make the swing from our gathering point in San Antonio,

Caravaners climb one of the buildings of Palenque, most beautiful of the Mayan Ruins.

Texas, to the far reaches of the Yucatán Peninsula. After we had seen the best of the Maya, we crossed over to the Pacific coast and climbed the mountainous backbone of Mexico to visit Oaxaca, Taxco, Cuernavaca and Mexico City on the way north to San Luis Potosí before returning to the states at Laredo, Texas.

Several caravan companies offer trips to the land of the Maya. One is offered by Tracks to Adventure, 2811 Jackson Avenue, El Paso, TX 79930, 1-800-351-6053. The price of their Yucatán tour is $4,275 (plus Mexican insurance) for two people for 43 days. To put the cost in perspective, note that this caravan provides 10 meals at special restaurants for each participant, plus 71 tours and events. Most importantly, it provides briefings by experienced wagonmasters to help you find your way and to make sure that you don't miss some of the sights. It includes the services of a tailgunner who will render emergency road service and make sure that you get to camp every night. The price also includes the services of a guide-linguist, a very valuable member of the team because of his or her ability to speak both languages and knowledge of where to find what you need.

The following is a day-by-day itinerary of a Mayan tour we knew about several years ago.

Day 1: Rendezvous in **McAllen, Texas,** briefing and get acquainted.

Day 2: Enter Mexico, overnight in **Ciudad Victoria** with full hookups.

Day 3: To **Tampico,** overnight and enjoy "Welcome to Mexico" dinner.

Day 4: Overnight at **Paradise Beach** with partial hookups. Sightsee banana and pineapple plantation.

Days 5 and 6:

In **Veracruz,** for sightseeing, time for shopping. Full hookups and tour of the city provided. See if you can talk your wagonmaster or guide-linguist into leading you to **Laguna Mandinga,** a freshwater lake just 7 miles south of the city. Here the shrimp boats come into the freshwater from the sea to unload their catch and—coincidentally—to kill the saltwater barnacles that attack their wooden hulls. I wonder if it is still possible to order a kilogram of the jumbo shrimp that we used to buy?

Day 7: Drive to **Graham Brothers' Ranch** in the country. Full hookups and special dinner provided. Most caravans to the

Yucatán stop for one or two nights at the trailer park known as "Ranchos Hermanos Graham," the ranch of the Graham brothers. Their park is off the highway, secluded, quiet— but the flares of the great oilfields act as a nightlight for the camp. No smell of oil, though. Please say hello for me to the brothers, Fernando and Guillermo. Although they are third-generation Mexicanos, they came from Scotland originally. Fernando had a short career as a minor league baseball player, and the whole extended family are good people and excellent campground hosts.

Day 8: Short hop to **Villahermosa,** a lovely big city with lots to see and do. Dry camp.

Day 9: Short drive to **Isla Aguada,** full hookups on tropical beach.

Day 10: Overnight in **Campeche.** Dry camp with rest rooms available. Walking tour of city.

Days 11 and 12:
Now you are in the land of the Maya. Dry camp right up against the fabled ruins of **Uxmal.** Light and sound show at night is terrific.

Days 13 and 14:
Full hookups in the city of **Mérida.** Sightseeing tour of very interesting city.

Days 15 and 16:
Two nights at **Chichén Itzá** (pronounced *Chee-chen Eet-zah*), one of the top three Mayan sites. Full hookups. Special Mayan buffet provided.

Days 17, 18 and 19:
Cancún. Your RV allows you to enjoy this fabulous resort where others pay as much as $250 per day to enjoy the same things. You'll be provided a sightseeing tour, plus a boat cruise of the harbor, breakfast and entertainment and a special dinner.

Days 20, 21 and 22:
Three days at **Chemuyil,** on the Caribbean Coast. Sightseeing tours to Mayan ruins of **Tulum** and to **Xel-ha** (pronounced *Shell-hah*). Surf fishing, snorkeling, tropical restaurant—relax under the tropical palms. This place can grow on you, and you may not want to leave.

Day 23: Overnight at **Bacalar,** a big freshwater lake. Dry camp.

Days 24, 25 and 26:

> **Palenque,** most beautiful of all the Mayan ruins, reclaimed from the green jungle that had hidden it for centuries. Full hookups.

Day 27: Return to **Rancho Hermanos Graham** and feel like you're back among friends again. Full hookups.

Day 28: Cross the isthmus to **Tehuantepec** on the Pacific Ocean. Showers and toilets available.

Days 29, 30, 31 and 32:

> Four fun days in **Oaxaca** (pronounced *Wah-ha-kah*) with full hookups. This is my favorite city in all of Mexico. Sightseeing tour by bus to the **Monte Alban Ruins,** where the ancient Indians leveled the top of a mountain for their ceremonial altars and other big buildings. Tour to the land of the black pottery makers. You'll be treated to a meal with entertainment. Offers one of the largest Indian markets in all of Mexico.

Day 33: Overnight in **Huajuapan de León** (pronounced *Wah-wah-pan*).

Days 34, 35 and 36:

> On to Cuernavaca, where the Aztec emperors lived during the summer. One of the best stops on the entire tour. Here, you'll have full hookups in a park overlooking the city. There'll be a bus tour to Taxco, home of the world's greatest silversmiths, a dinner in Taxco and another at Las Mananitas, one of the finest restaurants in the entire country. Lots of shopping opportunities here, especially for silver and leather.

Days 37, 38, 39 and 40:

> **Mexico City,** North America's largest city. Bus tour to **Teotihuacan**—greatest of all Aztec sites—with lunch provided. Sightseeing tour of the city, including another lunch at one of the city's finest restaurants. And best of all, you'll have reserved seats at the **Ballet Folklorico Nacional de Mexico**—which to my mind is the greatest stage show in the world. Fantastic colors and costumes, exotic rhythms and unbelievably good dance troupes make an unforgettable evening. I bought a videotape of the performance and nearly wore it out at home—until one of my grandchildren videotaped over it. With a population of about 23 million people,

the city has one of the worst cases of air pollution in the world, and horrendous traffic problems to go along with the eye-burning smog. If you have respiratory problems, they'll be worse here—but with all its faults, this is one of the most fascinating places on earth. If the time is right, you can take in a bullfight, you can tour the **Floating Gardens of Xochimilco** (pronounced *So-cheemill-coh*), visit the **National Pawn Shop,** travel past Mexico's national shrine to **Our Lady of Guadalupe** on a moving sidewalk! You should visit the Indian markets and take in some of the restaurants, among the best in the world. New excavations in the heart of the city have uncovered proof—as if any was needed—of the magnificence of the Aztec empire, which Hernan Cortez destroyed when he conquered Tenochtitlán—the Aztec City where Mexico City is now. As you walk by the famed cathedral in the heart of the city, you'll notice that this huge building is sinking slowly into the earth—which was once a great lake. Despite its shortcomings, Mexico remains the most interesting city on the North American continent. Please don't miss it!

Day 41:   Just a short hop to **Querétaro** (pronounced *Kay-ret-ahroh*) for an overnight stop with full hookups. Great shopping, especially for opals and other semiprecious stones. Take time to visit the **Hill of the Bells,** where Maximilian was executed.

Days 42 and 43:

At **San Luis Potosí,** full hookups in a pleasant trailer park. Walking tour of a very interesting city, plus a "Farewell to Mexico" dinner. At this dinner, you'll be entertained royally by the Estudiantina los Obreros or the Estudiantina Guadalupana—magnificent evening of music.

Days 44 and 45:

Full hookups at **Matehuala** with a fine restaurant available, plus a bus tour to the ancient silver mining town of **Real de Catorce.** You'll remember the bus ride through the tunnel.

Day 46:   To **Saltillo** for an overnight dry camp. Good shopping town if you have the urge.

Day 47:   Drive from **Saltillo** to **Laredo, Texas,** on good highways. Your caravan ends here, back home again.

If you are an experienced traveler and your rig is in good shape, there is no reason why you can't make this tour on your own or in a small group of two or three RVs. If you know a smattering of Spanish, it helps, but it surely isn't needed. You'll find someone to speak English all over Mexico these days, thanks to American movies and television. The biggest advantage of traveling alone is that you can set your own pace, while a caravan *must* stick to its schedule.

If you're traveling alone in Mexico, you'll find that the great majority of Mexicanos are friendly, helpful and honest. But there are a few "coyotes" who'll try to take advantage of you. Here are a few tips to prevent disappointment:

1. For gosh sakes, don't offer to pay for your gasoline by holding out a sheaf of bills for the station attendant to take his pick. You wouldn't do that back home, so why tempt the underpaid attendant in Mexico? Carry a pocket calculator and, while the attendant watches you, multiply the number of liters on the pump *(litros)* by the price per liter. Then get out your money and get as close to the exact amount as you possibly can. It's okay if you want to tip, but you don't have to.

2. Make sure your tires are in good shape when you leave the states, including your spare. Many tire sizes are not easily obtained in Mexico. I always carried a second spare lashed to the roof of my rig. I only needed it once—but that once paid for the extra effort.

3. Don't eat from street vendor carts—that is really asking for *la turista* otherwise known as "Montezuma's Revenge," a particularly virulent form of diarrhea. Carry along the nonprescription medicine Imodium, which is a sure cure for diarrhea. It is usually available in drugstores—*boticas* or *apotekarias* in Spanish.

4. Wash thoroughly any and all fresh fruits and vegetables purchased in Mexico.

5. Don't overdo your activity in Mexico; get your rest.

Most sickness experienced by travelers to Mexico is brought on by fatigue and dehydration. The climate is hotter than you're used to, so drink lots of fluids. Incidentally, Mexican beer *(cerveza)* is excellent in taste, but it won't help the dehydration problem. Fruit juices will, and Mexico has a dozen fruit juices you've never tried before. Mango and guayaba and strawberry and papaya—they're delicious!

The climate dictates that you make your Yucatán trip between the first of November and the last of March. This humid land can be frightfully hot and sweaty during the rest of the year. June is perhaps the hottest month, because it is dry heat. The rains start in July and continue almost unabated until late September. During this rainy season, much of the land is flooded, and today's Yucatecas think nothing of wading in 6 inches of water for several months of the year. This is especially true in the region of the lower Usumacinta River, which is far and away the biggest river in Mexico. During one late August trip, we piloted our motor coach along a blacktop highway, its edges marked by upright sticks standing in 6 inches of water—a huge lake that extended for more than 5 miles!

In December, January and February, the weather is ideal for RV camping, with clear skies sporting fleecy white clouds, very light breezes and almost no chance of rain. This is the best of the dry season, and is also the most insect-free time of the year.

Whether you go *en caravan* or independently, you'll see an entirely different culture from anything you've seen before—the wonderful world of the ancient Maya. Total mileage will be about 4,350 miles on roads ranging from wonderful to terrible.

Mists rise over the lush jungle that still hides part of Paleneque.

If you want to learn more about the parts of Mexico described in this chapter, you might be interested in reading:

Morley, Sylvanus and George W. Brainerd. *The Ancient Maya.* Stanford, California: Stanford University Press, 1983.

Vaillant, G. C. *Aztecs of Mexico.* New York: Pelican Books, 1955.

Krupp, Dr. E. C. *Echoes of the Ancient Skies.* New York: New American Library, 1984.

Luxton, Richard and Pablo Balam. *The Mystery of the Mayan Hieroglyphics.* Scranton, Pennsylvania: Harper and Row, 1981.

Avenie, Anthony F. *Skywatchers of Ancient Mexico.* Austin: University of Texas Press, 1980.

Henderson, John S. *The World of the Ancient Maya.* Ithaca, New York: Cornell University Press, 1981.

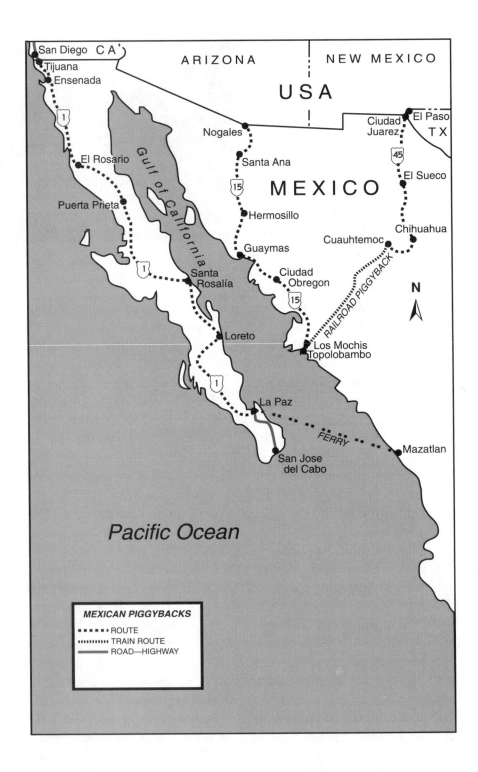

San Diego **C A**
Tijuana
Ensenada

A R I Z O N A

N E W   M E X I C O

U S A

El Rosario

Gulf of California

Nogales

Ciudad
Juarez

El Paso
T X

[45]

El Sueco

Santa Ana

[15]

M E X I C O

Puerta Prieta

Hermosillo

Cuauhtemoc

Chihuahua

Guaymas

Ciudad
Obregon

[15]

[1]

Santa
Rosalía

RAILROAD PIGGYBACK

N

Loreto

Los Mochis
Topolobambo

[1]

La Paz

FERRY

Mazatlan

San Jose
del Cabo

Pacific Ocean

MEXICAN PIGGYBACKS
▪▪▪▪ ROUTE
▪▪▪▪▪▪▪ TRAIN ROUTE
▬▬▬ ROAD—HIGHWAY

14
Piggybacking in Mexico, Single and Double

Single Piggybacks

Recreational vehicle travel into the sunny lands south of the border is as old as the RV itself. Travelers familiar with Mexico used their new RVs to further explore Mexico. But group travel—or caravaning—was another thing entirely. Some of the earliest caravans were those of Airstream. In very great numbers, Airstream caravans played follow-the-leader into the farthest reaches of Mexico. Priding themselves on being self-contained, Airstream caravans usually parked on soccer fields or along the sidestreets of some of

the larger cities. In some cases, their great numbers played havoc with the local people as they not only exhausted the supply of gasoline but also took on all of the potable water available in the smaller towns.

However, regularly scheduled large-scale touring of Mexican attractions really started with the legendary Gil Andrews. And it began with the "piggyback." Therein lies a story. The Vietnam War brought three young GIs to El Paso to study the Vietnamese language. Close friends Scooter Harding, Steve Steele and Gil Andrews fell in love with El

Paso and, more importantly, with everything Mexican. They made a pact that they would reunite after the war and go into some kind of business together. Gil Andrews was so proficient at the Vietnamese language that he was retained in El Paso as an instructor.

After the war, they started a business leading four-wheel-drive vehicles into the wilder country of northern Mexico. This evolved into a business of leading RV tours via the railroad, across the Copper Canyon to Los Mochis and into Mazatlán. Each of the three pledged to give it their best, come what may, for one year. They led their first tour, with only a few vehicles, in late 1971. I was on their second trip, in early 1972, with thirteen paying customers, if I remember correctly. That trip was written up in one of the RV magazines and things started to pick up as a result of advertising. But before the business really took off, the one year of testing was over, and Steele and Harding opted out of the agreement. After all, they had wives to support, while Gil was still unmarried. *Caravanas de Mexico* became the sole property of Gil Andrews, and he really went to work promoting his only tour offering. Called the "piggyback," this tour rendezvoused in El Paso and crossed the border under Gil's personal supervision. Border crossing had been

greatly facilitated by Gil's ability to handle the Spanish language with fluency. They drove south to the city of Chihuahua where they maneuvered their vehicles onto regular railroad flatcars. The vehicles were securely fastened down with heavy wire harnesses and huge blocks of wood were nailed down in front and back of each tire. Then the locomotive took over and the train moved west through the Mennonite farming country and up to the tiny mountain town of Creel. There an ancient Mexican bus took over and the travelers went down into the rugged canyon and visited the land of the Tarahumara Indians, one of the most primitive tribes in Mexico. The Tarahumaras are one of the most interesting of the hundred different Indian races in Mexico. Famed for their endurance, they still compete in a game of long-distance running while kicking a ball, and they may run as much as 100 miles at a time. Some of the piggyback caravans featured bus trips to Canyon Urrique, with emphasis on reaching the high lookout places where photographic opportunities were greatest. Other stops were in Bahuichivo and the Divisadero, where they looked down into the depths of the Barranca del Cobre, Mexico's Grand Canyon. Barranca del Cobre translates into Copper Canyon, and that geologic feature is about four times the size of the Grand Canyon, although it lacks the same fiery-colored cliffs and striking formations. Then the train crossed the Sierra Nevada Mountains for the long run down to sea level at Los Mochis. There the caravan drove off the railroad cars and went on to visit Topolobampo, Culiacán, Navajoa and the fun city of Mazatlán.

After three or four days of enjoying Mazatlán's great beaches, historic buildings and fascinating Indian markets, the caravan then drove the highways back to the United States via San Carlos Bay and Hermosillo before crossing the border at Nogales.

This tour was a great introduction to Mexico for RV travelers. It offered leadership that handled the language barrier very well, and it provided time to gawk at the scenery while someone else—the locomotive engineer—did the driving. Business grew and grew until the day arrived when a piggyback departed El Paso once a week from late October into March. Obviously it took more than one leader. Gil hired several wagonmasters to lead the tours and hired several more Spanish-speaking guides to handle business with the railroad authorities. Bill Wallace led at least nineteen piggybacks and then went into the office to handle the scheduling of the cara-

A caravan up the Baja Peninsula offers access to uncrowded campsites beside the sparkling sea.

vans. El Paso native Cesar Alonzo handled more of the guide jobs than anyone else. In addition to speaking Spanish better than the Mexicans, he was somewhat of a diplomat and very good at talking the caravans out of any problems they might get into with the railroad and state authorities.

There are drawbacks to any trip, of course, and the piggyback suffered from a lack of potable water available to the travelers. If you had a big enough holding tank and a big enough freshwater tank, you could enjoy the four days atop your private flat car. In fact, most travelers started out with the idea that they really had to stint on freshwater use and were surprised to find that they'd arrived at the next source of potable water with their tank half full. It's really amazing how little water we really need, if we're aware of the necessity to conserve. One wagonmaster, briefing his caravaners before they left El Paso, used to tell them that they needn't worry because "everybody smelled the same." In truth, it never seemed to be a problem for most rigs.

More RVers got their first taste of Mexico via the piggybacks than by any other method. Naturally competition sprang up and there is still a lot of competition for the railroad business. Larry and Maria Olsen's Tracks to Adventure started out as Tracks to Mexico, and they still provide excellent service over this route. The tour was accomplished in just eighteen days, about as long as many customers could afford, and it allowed the traveler to enjoy the rugged wonders of the mountain scenery while leaving the driving to the railroad engineers. Most of the people sat out on the flatcars in their deck chairs and enjoyed the spectacular scenery and bright sunshine at a pleasant 10 to 15 miles per hour.

This railroad, officially named El Ferrocarril Chihuahua al Pacifico, is unlike any other railroad in the world. On its path through the Bar-

ranca del Cobre, it becomes an engineering masterpiece. There are bridges spanning rivers as much as 350 feet above the riverbed, and you'll go through many tunnels carved out of the solid rock, the longest one more than a mile long. It's the recommended procedure to stay in your vehicle while going through the tunnels, but there are always some who prefer to sit on their lawn chairs and stare into the darkness. I've never heard of anyone being seriously hurt while making this journey, although I do remember one guy—who always knew better than anyone else what was good for him—who rode on top of his motor coach into the longest of the tunnels. In the absolute darkness, he decided that it was time to reload his camera. Sure of himself as always, he climbed down the ladder and headed for the door to his coach. Disoriented in the darkness, he stepped off the side of the flatcar. He hit the ground pretty hard and found himself lying beside the crossties, so decided correctly that the best course was to stay perfectly still. When the train passed, he started walking after it. His wife reported him missing as soon as the train cleared the tunnel and railroad authorities started walking back into the tunnel using flashlights to illuminate their path. I know that they must've dreaded what they would find, but they were overjoyed to meet him coming out. Other than a lot of black and blue marks, he was none the worse for wear. The moral is clear: Sit still, preferably inside your vehicle, while going through the tunnels.

Because it was so popular, the piggyback caravan grew into the business that now offers RV tours to all parts of Mexico and Central America, to the Canadian Maritime Provinces (see chapter 11), to most of Europe, to Australia and New Zealand, even side tours to Fiji, as well as river barge cruises down the mighty Mississippi (see chapter 9).

Although there have been many changes and improvements in the original piggyback tour, it still offers a quick and interesting introduction to Mexico at the lowest price possible. For more information call **Tracks to Adventure** at 1-800-351-6053. You don't even have to own an RV to enjoy some of this travel. Train trips in comfortable cars are now provided through the Copper Canyon. One of the most memorable trips of my RVing life was touring the Barranca del Cobre during Holy Week. You see, the Catholic faith was brought to the Tarahumaras in the early 1600s and really took root. But there was a period of several centuries when there was no priest to lead the Catholic worshippers among the Tarahumara. Re-

markably, they retained much of the true faith, but their beliefs took on strange new twists. For example, Judas became the most important figure in their re-enactment of the Holy Week pageant. The background music for their Lenten services was from drums and "cigar box" violins, yet they actually produced good sounds and the strange service was performed with great devotion.

Double Piggybacks

A natural outgrowth of the piggyback tour came when several companies began offering "double piggybacks." After leaving the initial driving to the railroad, RV travelers continue down to **Mazatlán** where they drive their RVs into the hold of a huge steamship operated by the Mexican government. It is forbidden to remain with your vehicle during the crossing, probably because of the air pollution from auto exhaust belowdecks. The traveler receives a numbered reclining seat, which is fairly comfortable to sleep in, or else buys a stateroom for more luxurious sleeping. There follows a nineteen-hour voyage across the usually placid **Sea of Cortez** to make landfall at **Pichilingue,** the ferry landing serving **La Paz, Baja California del Sur,** at the southern end of the Baja Peninsula. For many RV travelers, crossing the Sea of Cortez

The "Malecon," or beachside promenade, in Mazatlan, Sinola, Mexico.

is the high point of their journey. Porpoises gambol alongside the huge ship, whales are often in sight and thousands of seabirds wheel in the air above the ship.

Once on the Baja Peninsula, another aspect of multifaceted Mexico becomes apparent. The federal government has invested heavily in irrigation projects aimed at increasing production of food crops needed for the 80 million citizens of Mexico. North of this irrigated country, the RV caravan traverses the length of desert Baja all the way to San Diego, with intermediate stops at **Cabo San Lucas** (home of the world's greatest sport fishing) **Loreto, Guerrero Negro, Bahia Los**

Angeles, Ensenada and other trailer parks providing access to the spectacular sights of the Baja Peninsula. If the time is right, you'll make a side trip to watch whales in their breeding grounds at **Scammons Lagoon,** and you'll surely gain a new appreciation of the peace and solitude of this once feared road—where the Baja 500 was run for years. Roads have been greatly improved and, consequently, traversing the Baja is no longer a feat to brag about. However, it is still important to have your rig in excellent mechanical shape before you start out. Good tires are an absolute necessity, and you should carry a full set of spare belts, hoses and spark plugs if your rig uses them.

Several companies now offer the double piggybacks, and some of them even offer the trip in reverse, starting at San Diego and driving down the peninsula to ferry from La Paz to Mazatlán, returning north on Highway 15 to exit at Nogales.

It's hard to explain the lure of the Baja Peninsula. Although there are many who see it as a barren desert, others appreciate its own natural beauty.

15
Defensive Driving with Your RV

Our purpose in this chapter is to help you avoid damage to your rig by collision—either with another vehicle on the highway or with a picnic table at your campsite.

In seven years of leading assorted recreational vehicles into, through and back out of Mexico, we came to the conclusion that the two most dangerous words in the RV lexicon are, "Mom back!" As you've probably already figured out, "Mom back" is short for, "You come on back!" These deadly words, spoken by one spouse to another as he or she tries to guide the driver back into a camping space, have led to divorces, embarrassingly loud arguments disrupting their marrital bliss and more than one dinner begrudgingly prepared by an angry spouse.

All too often, the person walking behind and yelling, "Mom back!" is watching carefully for anything on the ground that the RV might hit, but neglected to watch *above,* where sturdy tree limbs can lie in wait for the motor coach or trailer that is happily "Mom backing!" into the space. Or perhaps they are gladly noting that the bumper and coach body are clearing a big rock, failing to notice that the muffler or gas lines are not. You might think I'm putting too much emphasis on maneuvering into the campsite, but long experience has taught me that this is when most of the dings and dents in your RV will occur.

A few tips are in order. First, the driver should position the rig in the correct place from which to start backing into the space and then get out and walk around the rig to look for unseen obstacles, determine how sharply he or she has to turn the wheels to back in smoothly and check to see what obstacles from the back limit the trailer space. The driver then returns to the driver's seat with a much more clear idea of what to do. That same walkabout inspection will show the driver where the connections are for water, electricity and sewer, helping him or her decide how far to back in to reach these facilities. This reconnaissance also lets the driver know where to stop the rig to put the open door in the best position and whether or not there will be room for the extended awning.

The helper then gets out and goes to the left rear corner of the coach in a position where the driver can see him or her clearly in the rearview mirror. By previous agreement, the helper knows that when pointing in a certain direction the driver will steer the *rear end* of the RV in that direction.

Having established visual contact with the helper in the rearview mirror, the driver begins to back *slowly* into the parking space. If the driver is moving too far to one side or another, the helper points in the direction the rear end must go and the driver gradually changes the angle of the front wheels. Whenever the vehicle is in motion, the helper should be walking close to the left rear corner of the vehicle, watching carefully for obstacles on the ground and overhead. It goes without saying that the helper should be very sure of his or her footing to avoid tripping or falling.

There are variations to this procedure, of course. One couple who traveled with us had a unique one of their own. She would get out of the vehicle, walk several hundred yards away and stay there while he expertly backed into the space. He was a former truck driver and she was a basket of nerves. It worked beautifully for them.

The most expert husband and wife teamwork I've ever seen was displayed by a delightful couple from the state of Washington. He was a retired captain in the U.S. Navy. She got behind the wheel and slowly started backing the rig—the key word is *slowly.* She never looked at anything except her husband's pointer finger as he walked in front of the tow car. If his upright finger pointed to the left, she turned the steering wheel to the left. When his finger returned to the perpendicular position, she returned the steering wheel to its former position. There was not a word spoken and the rig never stopped; it just slid smoothly into the proper position. When I complimented him on the operation, he explained, "It was developed to avoid a divorce."

Speaking of variations on this theme, Mexican truck and bus drivers use a system whereby the assistant walks to the left rear corner of the rig and pounds on the rig in a steady rhythm if everything is going smoothly. If the rearward course is in need of correction, the assistant simply stops thumping, the driver takes a careful look in the rearview mirror, takes orders from his assistant and makes the necessary correction. The fact that he makes no signal when something is wrong sounds backward to us, but it works and is used almost universally in Mexico.

If you are towing a car or a boat behind your coach, it goes without saying that you should disconnect the towed vehicle before attempting to back in. I once watched a man on Vancouver Island efficiently back his trailer, which was towing a boat. He did it well, but I wouldn't even attempt it. In fact, I believe such double tows should be illegal (as they are in several states).

If you have worries about the "backing in" process, it pays to ask for a pull-through space when you first go to register. Campground operators often find themselves without any pull throughs, so believe them when they say there are none available.

A second area of caution is the filling station. Once, in Shamrock, Texas, a filling station operator motioned repeatedly for me to come ahead. I worried that I might be too high for his shelter, but he kept on motioning for me to come ahead. I caught his eye and pointed to the top of the rig. He walked back a few yards, took a good look and motioned me to come on in. "Plenty of room," he called, just as the air conditioner on top of my coach smashed all of the fluorescent tubes in the overhead lighting fixture.

It is usually possible to find a station that offers easy access—in and out—so I drive past the "tight squeeze" places. The worst hazards at filling stations are the big metal posts installed around the pumps to prevent patrons from bumping into them. These posts are about 3 feet tall and are easily overlooked. They can sure put a nasty dent in your new RV.

On the Road

Now let's turn our attention to driving on the open road.

Obviously, a 30-foot motor coach takes longer to change directions than does a standard-sized auto. Driving a big rig requires different techniques, but even the rawest of new recruits quickly learns them. It soon becomes second nature to anticipate turns more, to turn in a big sweeping arc instead of a tight "jackknife" turn. You'll learn quickly that you have a lot of coach in back of you and must allow for the overhanging rear end when making turns. Length alone is not a hardship for the driver; it simply requires more careful attention to what you're doing than is necessary in a passenger car.

Width, however, is another story. Twice I've damaged my coach by forgetting that it is a lot wider than a passenger car. Both happened in construction zones when I tried to wheel my coach between the orange barrels. Cars whizzed merrily through ahead of me, and I didn't realize that highway construction crews do not place barrels for RVers' convenience, but for their own. In such cases it's a good idea to go very slowly. Then, if the gap isn't wide enough for your RV, you'll merely nudge the barrels out of the way instead of smashing into them and damaging your rig. Several times I've even stopped, ignoring the impatient honking behind me, and moved the offending barrels enough to let my rig through. It pays to be extra cautious around construction barriers.

For most newcomers to the RV life, eighteen-wheel trucks known as "semis" can be frightening. Much of this fear is generated by the "bow wave" or backwash of air as the big semi overtakes and passes you. If you see the truck coming in your rearview mirror and are ready for the bow wave, it doesn't bother you at all. But if you're half-asleep at the wheel and your rig is suddenly blown toward the roadside ditch, it can be very traumatic. Actually the push to the right is not very strong, despite what you feel at first. If you have a solid grip on the steering wheel, you probably won't have to correct at all—or at worst, make a very slight turn toward your left. The amount of the "push" increases with the height, or "sail area," of your vehicle. The taller your rig, the more the bow wave will affect you. If your rig has a very low profile, you'll hardly notice the push. Dual wheels on the rear help to minimize the perceived affect of the push. All in all, it's not something to worry about; it's simply something to understand and be prepared for.

The above applies to motor coaches and pickup-mounted campers, but trailers and fifth wheelers are different.

With the towed vehicle, the bow wave thrust obviously affects the towed vehicle before it is felt in the towing vehicle. If you're looking in the rearview mirror as the semi catches up to you, you'll probably see the rear end of the trailer move to the right. As the semi passes you, the bow wave tries to turn the front end of the trailer to the right. The cumulative effect of the bow wave here is to start the trailer "fishtailing," or swinging from side to side, instead of following the pulling vehicle in a straight line. The amount of "side sway" here is what we're concerned with. We want to minimize this fishtailing sway or eliminate it completely.

How?

First of all, have an antisway device installed on the front end of the towed vehicle, where it connects to the ball hitch. This essential piece of equipment is capable of removing 90 percent of the fishtailing, if applied properly. For every trailer tower, it will be money well spent. Any good RV service center will sell you one and install it properly. At the same time that you're applying the antisway device, make sure that your tow vehicle and trailer are level with each other and the road. In other words, if your trailer tongue weight makes the rear of the tow vehicle sag downward, sway will be increased. Leveling can be accomplished by means of air bags added to your springs, by increasing the size and strength of springs, or by changing the height of the ball hitch.

When you go about the business of leveling your truck and trailer, be realistic. Do the equalizing with the trailer fully loaded as it would be on the road, and with the tow vehicle also realistically loaded, including the weight of two adults and full gas tanks.

One last remark about trailer fishtailing: It has been my experience that a slight acceleration will stop the fishtailing and "snap" the trailer back into line. At times, however, there may be a vehicle ahead of you in your lane, which would obviously prevent you from accelerating. Stepping hard on the brakes will usually increase the fishtailing effect. Test the reaction of your own rig on the road when no one else is around by intentionally initiating the fishtailing and then accelerating to stop it.

Changing Lanes

Whether we like it or not, every RV has a blind spot behind it, a place where a tiny automobile can hide, undetected by careful glances in the rearview mirrors on both sides. At the present time I drive a 31-foot motor coach that has a spot directly behind it—and close to the coach—where a Volkswagen bug can hide. It's one of the great puzzles of life to me how, after checking both mirrors and then starting to change lanes to the right, a small auto will invariably dart out from directly behind me into that right-hand lane.

To minimize this problem—you can't eliminate it entirely—it is necessary to anticipate lane changes far ahead of time. At legal speed limits, use your turn indicators at least 500 yards before the anticipated lane change. Then look in both rearview mirrors before making the change. Once you're certain the right lane is clear, don't dawdle around. Your signaling has been adequate, and you should get the lane change over with right away—it isn't safe to slide halfway into the right lane and then hang there before claiming your new lane.

Rearview mirrors are important equipment for all RVs. They should measure at least 7 by 10 inches to provide a wide field of vision behind you. There are convex "fisheye" mirrors that can be mounted on or beneath the regular rearview mirrors to give you an even wider field of view. They're a great help in making sure that a small vehicle coming up fast behind you won't be overlooked.

When discussing lane changes, we've been assuming that you're driving on a divided road, perhaps an interstate highway, with plenty of lanes and no oncoming traffic. But is that realistic?

I feel that it is safer and less nerve-racking to use the interstates whenever possible. Lots of people disagree with me on that. My brother Ken, a long-time RVer, al-most never takes the interstates. He says that he wants to see the country, not fly through it with his eyes on the "super slab." Even those of us who like the divided highways have to get off them once in a while, just to get to where we're going. Which brings us to the bane of two-way traffic and the difficulty of passing safely. I know that your big rig probably has as much (or more) pickup than an economy class automobile. My coach is powered with a Chevrolet 454 and will accelerate with the best of them. But even if my acceleration is greater than that of a passenger car, I have to get a whole lot more vehicle *past*. It takes longer for a 31-footer to pass another vehicle than it does for a short car, right? So you have to allow for that length, which means you have to see farther ahead with your RV than you do with your passenger auto. That's obvious, but a lot of people don't keep it in mind. Here again, I want to emphasize that passing is no time for dawdling around. See your opportunity, signal and get moving. Don't swing out into the oncoming lane and ride there while you think it over. Get the pass over with in as short a time as you possibly can, and then get back into your own lane.

Use your best speed when passing, both to get it over with and to allow you to get safely ahead of the car you've passed before you have to cut back into the right-hand lane. Signal both when leaving your lane to pass and when returning to your lane. The polite RV jockey doesn't pass and then cut back in front of the vehicle being passed. If you force the vehicle to slow down, you're not a good driver, or you shouldn't have passed.

Lots of us like to make a leisurely trip out of it, to take time to smell the roses. That's great—maybe that's why you bought the RV in the first place. But if your leisurely driving means that a long line of vehicles is forced to crawl along behind you—that's not so great. If you notice more than two vehicles following you, unable to pass—please pick the first opportunity to pull off and let them pass. You have a right to set your own pace; you don't have the right to set the pace for others.

When you see a vehicle overtaking you and you know that it wants to pass you, it's a good idea to pull slightly to the right (as far as safety permits) to allow the overtaking vehicle to see ahead. This is simple courtesy, but it's also a safe driving habit that you should develop until it becomes second nature.

Come to think of it, courteous driving *is* safe driving.

16
The Fine Art of Grab-Sleeping

There's an old saying about us RVers that has perhaps more truth to it than humor: "An RVer is someone driving a $100,000 motor coach, towing a $15,000 car on a $1,000 dolly, looking for a place to camp free for the night."

Yet many of us feel that it is a God-given right to sleep in our self-contained rig without paying anyone for the right to park our bedroom on their land. Many of us rationalize this by saying, "It's not like we wanted to *camp* there; we just wanted to grab some sleep and be on our way."

Many years ago, my wife and I towed our Apache tent trailer (also known as a pop-up trailer) to the higher elevations of the Santa Fe National Forest. We arrived after dark and found the first few forest service campgrounds filled, so we drove on past the smaller ones which were also filled. Our two youngsters were getting tired and cranky, and we were getting desperate.

Then we saw a wide expanse of flat grassland, with no one around. We drove off the road onto this green lawn and quickly set up our home for the night. After a quick bite, the four of us rolled into our sleeping bags and slept the sleep of the innocent. In the early morning, my young son got up first and quickly re-entered the tent trailer to whisper, "Dad, I think we oughta get out of here. We're camped in the backyard of a house." We quickly folded our tent and silently stole away. I hope the owner of that inholding land never knew we were there.

And then there's my experience in a medium-sized town in Oklahoma. I was working away from home, and it so happened that the distance was much too great to allow me to drive home after work on Friday. But I could drive to this Oklahoma town and "grab a few hours of sleep" and then be on the way home Saturday morning to arrive before noon.

The first time I drove until about 10:00 P.M., arriving in Unnamed, Oklahoma. I found a level street in a residential district on a quiet section of town and turned off the lights to "grab some sleep." About 11:30 I was awakened by a patrolman pounding on my door. "You can't sleep here, buddy, this is residential territory. Move on!" He wasn't amenable to my sweet talk; he just repeated, "Move on!"

Bleary-eyed, I drove a couple of miles to the western edge of the small city and drove onto a vacant lot and turned in to "grab some sleep." I was awakened at about 2:30 by another uniformed patrolman banging on my door with the familiar, "You can't sleep here, buddy. Move on!" Disgusted, I moved on—about 40 miles westward and parked in a highway rest stop. By that time, I was no longer able to go to sleep, so I headed for home long before the sun came up. I was tired and angry.

Two weeks later, I came tooling into Unnamed, Oklahoma, again at about 9:00 P.M. After ascertaining that there was no trailer park in town, I went directly to the "overactive" police department.

I said, "I'm too tired to drive safely. There's no trailer park in town. I only want to grab a few hours sleep and then keep on going. What do you suggest?"

The man behind the desk answered quickly, "Four blocks west, turn to the right. Five blocks and you come to the big hospital. They've got a big parking lot north of the building which is usually completely empty at this time of night. Park on the north end of their lot and keep the noise down. No one will bother you!"

No one did. I slept until 5:30 in the morning and headed for home completely refreshed. I guess the moral of this tale is that the police are not always the enemy.

I've a friend named Ray. He and his wife are full-timers—they live aboard their RV and have no other permanent home. They almost never pay for camping privileges. Often they spend the night in supermarket parking lots. When I asked him if they were ever awakened by security patrols and told to move on, he grinned and said, "Yes, about once in ten, but the other nine times are free and we usually move to another free location when told to move." He's also been known to fill up at gas stations just before they close and to ask the station attendant for permission to park on station property for the night. He's a sound sleeper who doesn't mind traffic noise—or at least he claims he doesn't mind.

One of my fondest memories of the fine art of grab-sleeping happened on my very first trip into Mexico—must have been about 1962 or 1963. I knew only a few words of Spanish and the Mexican people were an unknown entity to me. Darkness overtook us a few miles north of San Juan del Rió, near the larger town of Hidalgo del Parral. In the darkness, I nearly hit a trio of burros who were lying in the middle of the road, savoring the retained heat in the blacktop. Many times I'd been told that it was suicidal to drive Mexican roads after dark, so I was anxious to get off the road—and I didn't care how. Creeping along in the Stygian blackness, I finally came to a side road, nothing but an opening in the sagging barbed wire fence, no building in sight. Gratefully I turned in, found a fairly level

place and turned off the motor with a sigh of relief. This was a big pickup camper, and we turned on the interior lights to prepare a meal. We were eating when we heard the unmistakable sound of hoofs on the blacktop just 50 feet from our "campsite"!

Opening the back door, I stepped out in the shaft of light from the camper. There was nothing to be seen, it was darker than a bear's belly, but the sound of hooves told me that the unseen visitors were turning in on "our" road.

"*¡Amistad!*" came a voice out of the darkness. I knew enough to realize that the unseen speaker was saying "friendship" in Spanish. I called back, "*¡Amistad!*" and listened as the sound of hooves faded away up the primitive road. We slept peacefully and didn't wake until morning when the local burros—jackasses sometimes called "mountain canaries"—began to serenade the morning's first light by braying.

We were eating breakfast when my daughter saw something outside. "Dad, there's a Mexican man and two little girls sitting out there watching us!" We left the breakfast table to go out and meet our visitors. The man stood up with a big smile, saying *"Buenos dias, señor y señorita."* After we shook hands, our newfound friends gave us a present of six chicken eggs.

I couldn't speak Spanish and he couldn't speak English, but we made ourselves understood. In English, I begged his pardon for trespassing on his land. (In the daylight, I could see his small home just 300 yards up that road.) I think he understood. In Spanish, he told us that we were most welcome and that he was happy to see us (I think). All of this was accompanied by many smiles and handshakes. My daughter lifted his two youngsters up into the camper so that they could see the inside.

Maybe that encounter was the real beginning of my love affair with the Mexican people. Thirty years later, I still love them.

Not all of my grab-sleeping occasions turned out so happily. Once we drove to the end of a road onto a spit of land extending out into Chesapeake Bay. It was lovely and quiet and very peaceful. We slept late the next morning and even went beachcombing before deciding to leave this idyllic spot. Driving off of the spit of land proved to be more difficult than driving in. Construction crews were plowing up the main road and had left a big ditch between us and the road! When I pointed out our predicament to the boss of the construction crew, he had a bulldozer brought down to level off the ditch and motioned us to go on through. When I yelled, "I might get stuck!" he retorted, "I just might have something strong enough to pull you out if you do!" That's the only time we've had the road cut off behind us when trying to grab a few hours of sleep.

Once a whole caravan of us nearly bought the farm at Playa Linda in southern Mexico, just up the coast from Acapulco. Our fifteen-rig caravan spent an idyllic three days on the beach there, swimming, snorkeling and just lazying around. Then the rains came. For twenty-six hours it poured cats and dogs. Our entry road disappeared under 2 feet of water and the exit turned into a bog. We cut palm fronds and laid them on the road so the lighter, smaller vehicles could get out. But there was no chance for the heavier motor coaches. However, our wagonmaster, Frank Hobbs, and our guide-linguist, Sergio Garcia, drove down the road and found a gravel truck hauling sand and rock to a building site. Sergio persuaded the driver to dump three loads of rock and gravel on the road—enabling the big coaches to crawl across.

Yes, we've had a lot of funny experiences while grabbing a few hours of sleep—by which we mean camping without paying. But times have changed and I've gotten thirty-five years older in the past thirty years. Nowadays I recommend against grab-sleeping. If you can possibly get to a campground, do it. It's money well spent. In fact, I've now gotten so conservative that I even recommend calling ahead to make a reservation for the next night.

I hate to admit it, but there are many places in the United States where it's simply not safe to grab-sleep. Violence and carjacking are on the increase and losing your money, possessions or even your life would be a big price to pay for saving a few bucks on campground fees. Remote and lonely campsites are attractive, but they're much safer when traveling in the company of other rigs. It is also more fun that way, for you have partners for bridge or any other activity.

I still use level spaces in Mexico to grab-sleep, more out of necessity than by choice. There are few real campgrounds in Mexico, simply because the RV season is so short that it is hard for a Mexican campground to make a profit. Also, I feel safer in most of Mexico than I do in the States. Exceptions are in the vicinity of the larger cities, where it is definitely not safe to camp out alone. I wouldn't grab-sleep near Mexico City or Acapulco any more than I would near Chicago or New York.

Whenever possible, I ask the "Green Angels," Mexico's wonderful tourist-helper police, for their recommendations on where to park. They've been very helpful.

I regret the passing of a safer era—a time when it was safe to park anywhere, and we didn't even lock the front door of our homes at night. It wasn't necessary. It is now, as I'm sure you'll agree. My recommendation is to camp in organized campgrounds at night—and to get acquainted with your neighboring campers whenever possible.

But if you're really in such a hurry that you just want to grab a few hours of sleep and then go on your way, use the roadside rest areas along our main highways. Some states even have "overnight" areas at their rest stops where you're a little farther from the rumble of big trucks; other states will run you out of their rest areas if you stop for more than a couple of hours. I've had some serious arguments with enforcement officers over the definition of the word "rest." Whenever I've insisted that I was just "resting" and not camping, I've been allowed to stay.

But if you want a good night's sleep without interruption, please use a real campground. The days of "grab-sleeping" seem to be gone.

17

The RV in Winter: Store It or Use It?

Living in New Mexico as I do, I don't feel the need to store my motor coach for the winter. I solve the "problem" of winter by using my coach all winter long. Sure, I sometimes go south with the birds, but I never stay the entire season. In fact, we're very traditional and spend Christmas and New Year's with family, and usually spend Thanksgiving at home.

Ours is such a beautiful, interesting world—so much to see and so few years in which to see it all. We operate on the assumption that sooner or later we'll no longer be physically able to travel, so we get in as much travel as possible while we still can.

We've used a pop-up tent trailer to camp in the dead of winter when the temperatures went down to 0 degrees Fahrenheit. We've used a pickup camper in the Rockies when the snow piled up so deep that we had to shovel a path for our truck through drifts. Despite the snow, we got in and we got out, and we had a lot of fun doing it.

One year in early November we used my 1985 model 31-foot Southwind as an elk-hunting camp. The temperatures stayed up at around 75 degrees in the daytime and only went down to 45 degrees at night, despite the fact that we were camped at an elevation of nearly

10,000 feet. That experience made us cocky. The next year we returned to the same place on the same dates but were met by temperatures of only 35 degrees for a high and well below zero at night, along with icy winds and 3 feet of snow.

No, nothing froze up, although we know we were lucky! We had taken lots of precautions. Our radiator coolant had been fortified and tested adequate for 15 degrees below zero. We tied a canvas tarpaulin around the front end of the coach to keep the frigid wind from going underneath the coach. We kept the curtains closed over the windows to hold in heat during the night and opened them to the weak winter sun during the day.

But the most important work had been done much earlier. We had put pipe insulation around all of our water lines beneath the cabinets and below the floor. And we didn't forget the "demand operated" water supply pump—being metal, it can freeze easily and crack open. We wrapped it with several layers of cloth, all fluffed up to provide "dead air space" around the pump.

We used our refrigerator to prevent food supplies from freezing, rather than to keep them cold— Mother Nature took care of that. Bulk supplies of items such as beer and potatoes were kept in large Styrofoam coolers and stored as high up as possible inside the coach. There's a big difference between the temperature at floor level and at ceiling level.

Like most hunting parties, we went out early in the morning and returned to camp for lunch and to rest up during the siesta hours before venturing out again for the prime hunting hours just before sunset. Within the limits of this regimen, we tried our best to make any heat-producer work double duty. We set the water heater at its highest setting, hoping the increased heat would help prevent the pipes from freezing.

When it was time to cook dinner, we started the motor coach generator and used the microwave to lessen the drain on our propane supply—which was hard hit by the furnace at night. Further along this line, we set the furnace setting about 5 degrees hotter than usual, to spread more heat a bit more often underneath the floor of our coach.

Finally, to keep the coach batteries, especially the ignition battery, at full strength, we fired up the Chevy 454 for half an hour just before going to bed. Residual heat in the exhaust pipes and mufflers helped delay the chilling effect of falling temperatures during the night.

We were quite proud of our heat management system, especially after we learned that a friend's similar coach, at the same elevation, had suffered burst water pipes during the coldest night. We felt quite smug until our friend pointed out the real reason for our better luck. We had been camped in the lee of a thick stand of conifers that sheltered us from the wind. Our friends had been parked in the open where the wind really got in its licks. The relentless fingers of the icy wind strip away residual heat, causing pipes to freeze.

One year later, we parked the same coach in the lee of the same stand of conifers, and this time we had added protection. We stretched three big tarpaulins to cover the space under the windward side of the coach, making it almost impossible for the wind to get a good crack at the tender underbelly of the coach. Temperatures went down to 8 degrees Fahrenheit every night during the four-day hunt, but nothing froze except the drinking water in my canteen.

I guess my message is that a motor coach doesn't freeze up as easily as you might think; the most important thing in preventing freezeups is to shield your pipes from the cold wind.

However, don't take chances and then write me a nasty letter if you lose. Recently, I took a brand new 27-foot Jayco motor coach on consignment for a trip from Albuquerque to Florida. Temperatures in New Mexico were freezing cold so we delayed filling the water tanks until we got far enough south into Texas that the nighttime temperatures posed no threat. Then, and only then, did we fill our tanks (filling and emptying them several times to get rid of most of the "new tank" taste in the water supply).

Now for a few directions on draining your water supply to avoid freeze-up. At the same time that you open your drain cocks, with the pump turned off, open all of the faucets in your coach. Letting air in at the top of the system will speed up the departure of water out the bottom.

Be sure you know where the "low point" drains are in your RV. Make sure the rental agency shows you where they are if it's a rental outfit, or the dealer when you buy a new RV. And in the unlikely event that the rig doesn't have "low point" drains, don't buy it. If you have an older model without such "low point" drains, I strongly recommend that you have one or two installed.

After you've drained all of the water down to the last drop, turn on your demand water pump to get rid of the last teaspoons of water that might have stayed in your pump. Even a very small volume of water freezing in a confined space can burst it apart.

When operating your RV in very cold weather, you'll probably run into some surprises. For example, we used the furnace a lot to keep the living area of our coach comfortable. But our rig had a privacy curtain that screened off the cab of the coach, so the driver's compartment got no heat at all. In the morning, we had solid ice, half an inch thick, on the bottom half of the windshield—on the inside! Warm, moist air had condensed and then froze on the icy windshield, at the same time that we were perfectly comfortable in the living space of our RV.

Freeze-proofing Your Water System

Almost every RV sold comes with instructions to flush the water from your water system and replace it with an antifreeze mixture during winter months. I did this just once, and despite rinsing the system with baking soda and other taste-removing substances, I couldn't get the taste out of my water tanks for months. For that reason, I never put antifreeze in my water system again. I prefer simply to drain the system completely when not in use or when the temperatures fall below freezing. If your RV service center insists on putting antifreeze in your rig, you'll have to make a decision. If you trust

the mechanic, and he assures you that the odor and taste can easily be removed, you may decide to try it. The choice is up to you.

There's good news these days for RVers who fear freeze-ups. Most popular RVs are now built with heat pipes and conduits routed through and around freezable water compartments. In one new model I looked at recently, the exhaust from the propane water heater was routed through the drinking water tank compartment, where it did a beautiful job of keeping the water temperature above freezing. But remember, you have four spaces to worry about: the drinking water supply, the hot water tank, the gray water storage and the sewage water storage. If you live in one of the northern states or plan on traveling in temperatures that are below freezing, make sure that all four sources of "freezable water" are protected. If you are buying a new rig, ask the salesperson about the "anti-freezing" features of the rig. If it doesn't have a heat transfer system such as the one I've just described, don't buy it.

And remember that these "anti-freezing" methods don't work when your furnace and water heater are turned off!

18
Full Time in Your RV

If you've enjoyed a recreational vehicle for any length of time, the thought has no doubt occurred to you that it might be a good idea to sell your home and move into your RV for keeps. Be a full-timer!

It sounds like an idyllic existence, and full-timing is indeed *the* life for many retired couples. I know one couple who retired from the army twenty-seven years ago and have lived full time in their motor coach ever since. For the first twenty-four of those years, they lived in a very small motor coach—I think it was a 22-footer—and only recently have they given in to temptation and bought a larger rig.

Another couple of full-timers bought their rig in southern California and sold their home there—effectively burning their bridges behind them. They drove no more than 300 miles on any one day, camped in forest service campgrounds whenever possible, and filled and drained their tanks at wayside stops. They moved slowly up through northern California, Oregon and into the Puget Sound area. By that time the winter was coming on and they bailed out—heading for warmer climates. That first winter they traveled the beaches of Padre Island, Texas, then moved slowly along into the bayou country of Louisiana.

When spring arrived, they traveled north along the Mississippi to Minnesota and—but you get the idea. The point is that they accomplished the move from their conventional lifestyle to the nomadic life of full-time RVing without once looking back

Bill and Margaret, on the other hand, thought that full-timing would be heaven. They sold their beautiful four-bedroom home, bought a big motor coach and hit the road. Within sixty days they were back in their hometown, had sold the RV and bought a small retirement home. They were sick and tired of the nomadic life.

Why do some full-timers love the life and others hate it?

Would *you* like the full-time life?

Before you decide, take an RV and hit the road for an extended trial. If you don't have an RV, rent one; but don't go into the full-time life without trying it first. The length of a full-time trial should be at least six months. Then, and only then, if you are still in love with the life, go ahead and become a full-timer.

To help decide whether or not full-timing is right for you, consider the following questions:

Do you and your spouse get along in cramped quarters, or do you get on each other's nerves once in a while and need to have your own space?

Do you carry on a correspondence with several old friends, and is it important to you? No matter what arrangements you make, your mail delivery will be sporadic and unpredictable.

Do you see your children and grandchildren often, and is that important to you? Full-timing will take you away from them, and you won't see as much of their growing up. For some people this is torture, for others it is a pleasant release from familial duties.

What are your main interests and hobbies? If you're a bird-watcher, angler, hunter, hiker, canoeist or photographer—that's a big plus, for your opportunities will be multiplied. But if your main interests are church, social work or other community-related activities you'll have to think carefully before becoming a full-timer. You'll have to sever many social ties, which can be very difficult for some people.

Are your finances sufficient to handle the major expense of buying gasoline? Remember, a motor coach gets only 7 to 10 miles per gallon, and it may be more than 2,000 miles between your seasonal destinations. That's 225 gallons of gas. Unless you want to make do with more rustic facilities, you'll be staying in trailer parks costing anywhere from $7 per day in Marfa, Texas, to as much as $38 per day in Key West. That's per day, my friends. In other words, there are plenty of expenses involved in full-timing. Don't underestimate the cost.

Are you capable of eliminating unnecessary things from your home on wheels? Are you the kind who likes to keep the daily newspaper for future reference, or do you throw it out the same day you buy it? Space is limited, no matter how big your RV, and full-timers are not allowed the luxury of being pack rats!

Do you feel restless and claustrophobic when foul weather keeps you cooped up inside your RV for days at a time? Or do you just curl up with a good book and enjoy yourself?

Would you be interested in part-time or occasional full-time employment during the course of your full-timing? There are many opportunities—if you search them out—to do simple jobs in return for a trailer site with full hookups. For example, you can sign up to be a campground host for the National Park Service or U.S. Forest Service. No pay, but easy work and a free campsite. Such employment can be a grand opportunity to meet interesting people.

Are you handy or mechanical enough to fix things when they need repair? If not, you're not a good candidate for the full-timing life. Of course, you can hire mechanics for every repair job, but you'll find them mighty expensive and you'll lose a lot of time. If you're not mechanically inclined, you can make up for it by taking courses in automotive repair, electrical wiring and so forth at your local community college or vocational training school.

Here let me repeat once more— try it out before you burn your bridges behind you. Rent out your home, or have a friend or relative housesit for you while you head into the unknown. If you find yourself calling home every few days to find out how things are going, full-timing is probably not for you. Are you really willing to sever the ties that bind and head into a new life?

Full-timing Mechanisms

Okay, you went and did it. You're now a full-timer. There are still a few problems to be solved, such as how to get your mail forwarded to you on the road. The best deal is to have a trusted friend or relative back home pick up the mail every day, weed out the stuff you don't want and then forward the rest to you— either at set intervals or in response to your telephoned instructions. Be very selective in choosing the person to handle this onerous task because it does get to be quite a chore, and each of us has different criteria as to what we want and don't want forwarded to us.

There are many mail-forwarding services available to full-time RV travelers. For example, **Travelers Remail Association,** 6110 Pleasant Ridge Road, Arlington, TX 76016, 1-800-666-6710, will forward your mail to your specifications and also provide an emergency locator service.

Some others are **Fast Forward Remail Service,** P.O. Box 917729, Longwood, FL 32791, 1-800-321-9950. The **Mail Travel Services,** 779 East Merritt Island Causeway, Merritt Island, FL 32952, 1-800-723-0110. **Snowbird Mail and Messages,** P.O. Box 0710, Newport, OR 97365, 1-800-800-0710. **Mail Forwarding Services,** P.O. Box 190, Jefferson, OR 97352, 1-800-452-2130.

Before engaging a mail-forwarding service, shop around, compare the prices and services you'll receive, for they vary greatly.

Some mail-forwarding services blatantly remind you that they operate in a state that has no state income tax and that using their address for your address can help you avoid taxes. Honesty is by far the best policy here, and there have been some real horror stories about full-timers claiming a tax-free address while actually voting and residing in another state. Don't plan on cheating the tax people, folks, it just isn't worth it.

The same word of caution applies to licensing your full-time RV. If you license it in state B which has a low tax, when your legal residence

is actually in state A, and you get caught—look out. The penalty can far exceed any savings you've made by misrepresenting your residence to pay lower license fees.

Another option is voice mail messaging, where you can call in to receive telephone messages from friends, relatives and business associates. One such operation that I am familiar with charges a $10 start-up fee, $10 per month and 24¢ a minute for use of the service. Pardon my cynicism, but if you need to stay in this close touch, full-timing is probably not for you.

The latest fad in communication for full-time RVers is electronic mail, whereby you use your own computer to access various networks, some free, some quite expensive, but all offering the luxury of almost instantaneous communication with the entire world of electronic mail.

Handling the Finances

Getting money into your checking account is relatively simple. If you don't already receive your retirement, pension or Social Security checks through direct deposit to your checking account, you should arrange this at once. Direct deposit is far safer than using the mail, and it is always on time. Other, nonperiodic income deposits are probably best handled by you through the mail, unless you have a trusted agent back home who will do this for you.

Making use of the money in your checking account isn't quite so simple. For good reason, banks and merchants are increasingly reluctant to accept personal checks from people they don't know. In the old days, a letter of introduction from your bank was sufficient to gain you check-cashing privileges, but this is no longer the case.

Today, a credit card is more readily accepted than the best check. It's almost impossible to full-time without using plastic. With your Visa or MasterCard, you can pay for camping privileges, gas and oil, entry to Disney World, new tires, repair work and get cash advances for things your credit cards don't cover. It is also possible to have your monthly bill and statement of transactions sent directly to your bank and have them pay it in full upon receipt. This works out well if you're operating with a comfortable margin between income and expenses. But if you're living from one paycheck to the next, this simply won't work. Overdraft charges will quickly ruin your working arrangement with your bank.

If you prefer, you can pay your own credit card bills when they are forwarded to you. One problem with this when full-timing is that you may find yourself paying interest charges, simply because the bill didn't reach you until after the deadline to "pay in full without interest." It's a good idea to discuss the handling of your credit card payments with your banker or financial adviser.

I can't recommend the use of travelers checks, because they're too expensive. Usually you will be charged 3 percent of the total value of the checks when you buy them. The idea of buying a large dollar amount of travelers checks is simply bad economics. You must realize that when you buy travelers checks, you're lending your money to the issuer of those checks without being paid any interest. In fact, unless you are a valued customer of the issuing office, you'll even be charged for the privilege of lending your own money to the bank.

In our situation, we have a neighbor who picks up our mail and puts it in our vacant home. At the end of each month, my son drops by, sorts out the bills and pays them. This works fine for us on those occasions when we're away from home for a month or longer, but it wouldn't work so well for actual full-timers.

There is no single answer to handling the finances while you're on the road; you'll have to find the solution that works best for you.

Bill and Janice sold their home and put the $150,000 in the bank.

They already owned a big fifth wheeler. They return to their hometown once a year—not at the holidays—but when it's time to file their income taxes. They almost never write letters; they keep in touch with a few relatives by telephone once a week. They don't have their mail forwarded. "It's not worth looking through, anyway," they explain. Sound too drastic for you?

In the last five years, Bill and Janice have visited every state in the union and every province of Canada. They spent five months exploring Alaska. They fell in love with the Florida Everglades and spent a month there each winter. Now they're turning their attention to Mexico and have plans to spend three full winters there. They enjoy U.S. Forest Service campgrounds where expenses are very low, and they have established a very happy lifestyle. Bill has resurrected a lifelong interest in fine photography and can now spend hours waiting for the clouds to be in exactly the right position to enhance a landscape. Janice says she has almost caught up on the reading she never had time for while raising a family and caring for a home. Both of them enjoy hiking and fishing. They've dined on trout and grayling from the Yukon, salmon and halibut from Alaska, bluefish and sea trout from the Carolinas, striped bass from Maine and Nova Scotia and tried to catch giant tuna in the offshore waters of Prince Edward Island. Didn't catch a tuna, but Bill says there's plenty of time for another crack at them. Incidentally, they both get complete physicals once a year and their health has never been better.

The moral is that full-timing can be heaven for some people—but not for others. You'll want to give it a realistic, long-term tryout before you sell your home and hit the road full-time.

Appendix

Favorite Campgrounds

Some campgrounds stand out in memory—some because they are beautiful, some because they are isolated and completely free of humanity. Some are historic, others are just plain fun.

Here are some campgrounds I've enjoyed, chosen from thousands we've camped in during the last thirty-five years of RVing. All were great when we camped there—but times change and nothing is guaranteed. But if you're in the vicinity, you might have a look.

Circle Up Campground, DuBois, Wyoming, (307) 455-2238. I remember this place fondly, having stayed there many times on trips to and from Grand Teton National Park. Maybe it is because I was hot and tired after the long drive and this park offers a wonderful indoor swimming pool. I always enjoyed a long cooling swim out of the sun. This park has continued to improve over the years, better each time I stopped.

West Bay Marina and RV Park, Victoria, Vancouver Island, British Columbia, Canada. A small but excellent campground right on the water's edge, served by small ferry boats that take you across to the city center. Well laid out and clean, and an excellent headquarters from which to explore Victoria.

KOA, Pensacola/Perdido Bay, Florida, 1-800-562-3471. Lots of room, lots of shade, lots of Spanish moss hanging from two-hundred-year-old oak trees. The first time we visited, we came in when it was already dark. About two hours later, a full moon came up, sending shafts of bright moonlight through the hanging moss streamers. We strolled through this surreal setting, admiring the long silver path across Perdido Bay lit by the moon. Very quiet, very nice.

Bahia Escondido, on the Baja side of the Sea of Cortez. There was no real campground, just an old crumbling concrete pier that was used to load cattle aboard tramp steamers thirty years ago. Not a soul around for the three days we stayed there. Didn't see a jet contrail or hear an airplane overhead. But we did catch a ton of scrappy fish, casting from the pier, broke huge oysters off the rocks at low tide and dug succulent clams from the mud flats across the bay. On a second trip there, we met a trio of Long Beach policemen who were traveling in a jeep, towing a tiny trailer that held their camping tents and sleeping bags as well as their fishing gear. We were all running short on supplies so we teamed up—they drank our cold beer and we used their onions and catsup. Added up, we had enough of everything for all five of us. We had to leave when we ran out of drinking water as there wasn't any to be had for 30 miles.

Cimarron or McCrystal Creek Campgrounds, Carson National Forest, New Mexico, (505) 758-6200 or (505) 586-0520. These are at 8,500 feet, and we camped there often while elk hunting with the muzzleloader. The motor coach made a fine base camp, but what I liked best were the panoramic vistas of bright yellow aspen-clad mountains interspersed with the dark green of the conifers. Quiet, lonely—wonderful. Night music was furnished by coyotes who seemed to resent our presence. It got so cold at night that we worried about freezing our water lines, but the afternoons were so hot we went around in short sleeves. I hope the good Lord lets me camp there a few more elk seasons.

Chemuyil, Yucatán, Mexico. We used to lead caravans into this idyllic spot on the seacoast south of Cancún, but now there's a hotel and no place to camp. We camped under the tall palm trees, just 50 feet from the serene blue ocean. Swimming was wonderful, but you had to steer clear of weed patches on the ocean bottom because there were sea urchins in the weeds and their needles inflict painful wounds. The ocean temperature was delightful, and they sold beer in a tiny cantina—usually warm beer. But progress has eliminated this one, which used to remind us of the old Dorothy Lamour movies with Bing and Bob.

Muncho Lake, British Columbia, Canada. Between Fort Nelson and Watson Lake on the Alaskan Highway, there are secluded campsites near the shore of a long narrow lake filled with very cold water. The silence is so complete that you rejoice when it's broken by the far-off call of a loon. Even in August, you'll sleep under woolen blankets—like an innocent babe.

Playa Azul, north of Acapulco on the Pacific Coast. Not much of a campground, but what a location! We camped on the beach years ago, probably can't do that nowadays. Small restaurant with authentic Mexican cuisine, including shrimp cooked in a hot pepper sauce. It brought tears to my eyes, but after the first searing mouthful, it was delicious.

Seward, Alaska, seashore. Operated by the city of Seward. We lined up our RVs facing the quiet waters of the Gulf of Alaska. Accommodations are quite primitive, but you have access to the Kenai Fjords National Park, to boat tours of the sound and to silver salmon fishing right off your doorstep. At this spot many years ago on Good Friday, an earthquake opened up a crack in the earth that swallowed railroad cars then closed back over them. But that only happened once, and we've camped there many times. While you're there, treat yourself to a boat tour or a charter fishing trip—the halibut are big and a thousand times better than the frozen variety you buy at home.

Lake Sakakawea State Park, on Garrison Reservoir, North Dakota, (701) 487-3315. Camping sites are very far apart, easy to get into and out of, all utilities are in perfect locations and there's a fine campground store. The lake is famed for walleye fishing and for a salmon fishery. In the summertime's hottest day, it seems that there's always a cooling breeze because this campground is surrounded on three sides by the huge, sprawling reservoir formed by Garrison Dam. They also have solar- and propane-heated water in the clean showers. Quiet and peaceful.

Corps of Engineers Campground, just below Oahe Dam, South Dakota, (605) 223-9805. Conveniently placed and well laid out, this big campground offers everything you need for RV camping, plus proximity to the best fishing on the entire "Great Lakes of the Missouri," for salmon and walleyes and northern pike. It's just a fifteen-minute run to South Dakota's capital city of Pierre (pronounced Peer not Pee-air because it derives from the Norwegian *Peer,* as in *Peer Gynt,* but the early map makers couldn't spell in Norwegian).

KOA Clewiston/Okeechobee, Florida. A friendly atmosphere and lots of activities make this one of the most pleasant stops in the Sunshine State. Close to Okeechobee's black bass fishing. See the chapter about Florida for details.

Sunny Sanctuary, Port Hardy, Vancouver Island, British Columbia, Canada. Big, wide open sites, all hookups, hot showers and clean rest rooms, this campground is memorable for the dozens of rabbits that keep the lawn mowed and for the wild Canada geese that spend their summers on the Quatze River, which forms the back border of the campground.

Motel Bahía Kino Campground, Old Kino, Mexico. About 75 miles west of Hermosillo on the shores of the Sea of Cortez, this is a very large, fairly well-kept-up place with shaded covers over your motor coach door. All hookups, good

showers with (not always) hot water. Access to excellent fishing via
two launching ramps—one on either side of the dark rock headland
that separates the sea from Kino Bay.
Lots of snowbirds spend their winters here, and there are a lot of organized activities run by the "Anglos"
who winter here. I started going
there before the park was built, more
than thirty years ago.

Group Caravans for RVs

There are many companies offering organized group caravans for
RVs. This is a partial list of RV or-
ganizations.

Alutiiq RV Adventures
P.O. Box 211242
Anchorage, AK 99512
1-800-426-9865

Creative World Rallies and Caravans
4005 Toulouse Street
New Orleans, LA 70119
1-800-REC-VEES
In Louisiana, (504) 486-7259

Foretravel Motorcade Club
1221 N.W. Stallings Drive
Nacogdoches, TX 75961
(409) 564-8367

Woodall World of Travel
6756 South Greenville Road
P.O. Box 247
Greenville, MI 48838
1-800-346-7572

Holiday Rambler Club
P.O. Box 587
Wakarusa, IN 46573
(219) 862-7330

Points South RV Tours
11313 Edmonson Avenue
Moreno Valley, CA 92555
1-800-421-1394

Tracks to Adventure
2811 Jackson Avenue
El Paso, TX 79930-9985
1-800-351-6053

Winnebago Itasca Travelers
P.O. Box 152
Forest City, IA 50436
(515) 582-6874

Foreign RV Travel

Recreational vehicle caravan travel
needn't stop at the ocean's edge. In
fact, hardly any part of our fascinating world is safe from the curiosity
of caravaning RVers, as well as those
independent characters who go it
alone.

For example, Creative World
Rallies and Caravans, 4005 Toulouse
Street in New Orleans, LA 70119, 1-
800-732-8337, offers a thirty-five-day
European caravan touring Germany,
Austria, Switzerland, Lichtenstein,
France and Italy. This tour is timed
to allow you to visit Munich during
Oktoberfest, which is one of my fa-

vorite happenings in the whole world. This caravan employs rented motor coaches (called "caravans" in most of the world outside of North America).

There are other companies offering overseas caravans, but they change from year to year. If you are interested in the subject, check the advertisements in *Trailer Life* and other RV magazines. However, I strongly urge that you do business with long-established companies that will be there after the caravan as well as when it is time to collect the money. It's also a very good idea to ask for references from travelers who've already made the tour. Contact them and ask the hard questions.

Driving a caravan in a foreign country is very different from RVing in our country. Have you ever driven on the left side of the road? Some people adjust without any problems, but some have a hell of a time getting accustomed to doing things on the southpaw side of the road. Count me as one of those who *hates* driving on the left side. I have a tendency to ride out a little toward the center of the road when there is no traffic. Then when an oncoming vehicle shows up ahead, I instinctively pull to the right—and that can get you killed.

Remember, too, that you don't take your own rig overseas with you, but rather rent European rigs. Which side of the cockpit do you suppose the steering wheel is on? I had a problem in Ireland. Every time I went to turn on the turn signal, I set off the window washers instead. If I had an Irish pound for each time I tried to get in on the left side instead of the driver's (right) side, I'd have enough money to buy a new motor coach.

With the notable exception of Germany's autobahn and a few Scandinavian roads, Europe's highways don't lend themselves to high-speed travel. If you want to visit the famed churches, art museums and other attractions of Europe, you'll have to visit them via bus, because parking is at a premium everywhere. Don't drive your motor coach onto the Champs Elysées in Paris or you'll risk the damnedest traffic jam (of your creation) you've ever seen. European cities were laid out centuries before the motor car was invented and they definitely are not designed for RV travel. Please don't interpret the above as an argument against RVing Europe. Take it as a warning that things are very different and that you should be very sure your tour includes bus transportation to the attractions. Don't buy a tour that tells you to go to a certain campground 25 kilometers from the cathedral and then blithely adds that you tour the city on your own.

While I'm being pessimistic, let's add another fact. The cheapest, and best, way to travel in Europe is on those wonderful trains. If you buy a Eurail Pass here in the United States—before you go overseas—you can travel from city to city on clean, fast, punctual trains, walk to your lodgings and eat in fine restaurants for a total cost that is much lower than the cost of a rented caravan tour. To replace the services of a guide, buy a book such as Arthur Frommer's *Europe on Fifty Dollars a Day*. When I first started traveling to Europe, the book's title was *Europe on Ten Dollars a Day*, which was more attainable at that time than today's $50 per day.

There's also the matter of campgrounds. Don't expect to find KOAs across the ocean; they aren't there—yet! For the reasons I've just listed, Europeans don't take to RVing with the same enthusiasm that we do. Their trains are a thousand times better than ours, their roads are not like our interstates and parking is almost nonexistent in a city of any size. So RVing in Europe is not as practical or as popular as here at home.

But if you're determined to "caravan it" in Europe, more power to you. Just be sure to get answers to all of your questions *before* you go, and be sure to check references from those who've gone before you.

Index

Travel Notes